SODA POP

Science Fair Projects

Thomas R. Rybolt

Enslow Publishing
101 W. 23rd Street
Suite 240
New York, NY 10011
USA
enslow.com

This book is dedicated to Jaxon and Caleb Hart— the next generation.

Acknowledgment

I appreciate the help of my children—Karen, Megan, Ben, and Leah—in developing and testing some of the experiments and the work of students in my 1998 and 1999 Honors General Chemistry classes who investigated carbonated beverage properties.

Disclaimer: Products and company names used are the trademarks of their owners.

Published in 2016 by Enslow Publishing, LLC
101 W. 23rd Street, Suite 240, New York, NY 10011

Cataloging-in-Publication Data
Rybolt, Thomas R.
  Soda pop science fair projects / by Thomas R. Rybolt.
    p. cm. — (Prize-winning science fair projects)
  Includes bibliographical references and index.
  ISBN 978-0-7660-7024-0 (library binding)
  1. Carbonated beverages—Juvenile literature. 2. Science projects—Juvenile literature. 3. Soft drinks—Experiments. I. Rybolt, Thomas R. II. Title.
  TP630.R93 2016
  663'.62—d23

Printed in the United States of America

To Our Readers: We have done our best to make sure all Web site addresses in this book were active and appropriate when we went to press. However, the author and the publisher have no control over and assume no liability for the material available on those Web sites or on any Web sites they may link to. Any comments or suggestions can be sent by e-mail to customerservice@enslow.com.

Portions of this book originally appeared in the book *Soda Pop Science Projects Experiments With Carbonated Soft Drinks.*

Illustration Credits: Accurate Art, Inc. c/o George Barile.

Photo Credits: Givaga/Shutterstock.com, p. 3 (pouring cola); Ohn Mar/Shutterstock.com (science background throughout book).

Cover Credits: Givaga/Shutterstock.com (pouring cola); Ohn Mar/Shutterstock.com (science background).

CONTENTS

INTRODUCTION

A large supermarket has thousands of cans and bottles of soft drinks available for you to buy. Which brand is the best-selling? Coca-Cola. Each year, the Coca-Cola Company sells the equivalent of about 410 billion 8-oz servings of soda pop and other beverages!

You may drink colas and other sodas, but what does that have to do with science? This book uses colas and other carbonated beverages as a way to explore science. This collection of science experiments and activities can be done alone or developed into science fair projects. After some fun with these experiments, you might learn to see every can or bottle of soda both as a drink you can enjoy and as a small laboratory waiting to be opened and explored.

History

Many carbonated beverages, especially colas, became popular in the late 1800s. Coca-Cola was one of them. In 1886 in Atlanta, Georgia, a pharmacist named John Pemberton developed a new drink based on ingredients he had extracted from the kola nut and coca plant. He arranged to have his drink sold at Jacob's Pharmacy, the largest pharmacy in Atlanta.

At the time, many pharmacies had soda fountains where people would have drinks made and served. Frank Robinson, Pemberton's partner and bookkeeper, suggested the name Coca-Cola since the drink came from the coca plant and kola nut. Coca-Cola was a hit with customers. Asa Candler bought the rights to Coca-Cola in 1891. Soda fountains around the United States began selling carbonated Coca-Cola.

In 1894, Joseph Biedenharn set up a machine in his pharmacy to bottle Coca-Cola so that people could drink it at places other than soda fountains. Carbon dioxide gas was forced under pressure into water to make carbonated water. The bottles were sealed so that the gas could not escape until the bottle was opened.

In 1899, Benjamin Thomas and Joseph Whitehead in Tennessee obtained the rights to bottle Coca-Cola nationwide. Along with Whitehead's new partner, Jack Thomas Lupton, they developed a system of independent bottlers who paid for the cost of building the factories to bottle Coke. The Coca-Cola Company supplied the Coca-Cola syrup, and the bottlers mixed the syrup with carbonated water.

In 1919, Mr. Candler sold the Coca-Cola Company to Ernest Woodruff for $25 million. Woodruff's son Robert Woodruff became president four years later. In 1928, Coca-Cola was the first drink to be sold at any Olympics. Robert Woodruff, who was active with the company for sixty years, helped to spread the drinking of Coca-Cola around the world. The Coca-Cola Company developed and introduced many other carbonated drinks, including Fanta in 1960, Sprite in 1961, TAB in 1963, Mr. Pibb in 1972, Mello Yello in 1979, diet Coke in 1982, Surge in 1997, Vanilla Coke in 2002, Coke Zero in 2005, and Coca-Cola Life (sweetened with stevia and sugar) in 2013.

As the Coca-Cola Company developed and expanded, other companies did too. Many other companies make a variety of colas and other carbonated soft drinks that compete with the Coca-Cola Company's beverages. Today hundreds of different carbonated drinks are bottled and sold around the world.

How to Use This Book

Each chapter in this book has an introduction to a topic, followed by three or four main experiments. Each experiment will expand your knowledge of the chapter topic. The experiments do not have to be done in any special order. You can skip around in the book to find the chapters that interest you most. However, you should read the chapter introduction before you perform any of the experiments in that chapter.

A section at the beginning of each experiment lists the materials you will need. The materials are all common items in your home or for sale at a grocery store.

At the end of each experiment, you will find a section called "Project Ideas and Further Investigations" that contains suggestions for additional experiments. You can use the original experiments or suggested further experiments as a great starting point to develop your own science fair project. Some of the initial activities are brief and are intended to be developed further in order to have a complete science fair project.

You should use a science notebook when you are doing experiments. Any notebook with bound pages—such as a spiral notebook—will do. You should always record the date, a description of what you are doing, and all your data and observations. If you are working on a science fair project, your notebook will be an important source of information to show your teacher and judges the work you have done.

In this book you will learn more about carbonated beverages. You will learn to see that every sealed carbonated beverage bottle and can is a tiny laboratory of liquid, gas, sugar, sweeteners, acid, coloring, and more—all waiting to be explored. If you want to enjoy a rewarding and refreshing science experience, grab a soda and come along.

The Scientific Method

When you do a science project, especially one with your own original research, you will need to use what is commonly called the scientific method. In many textbooks you will find a section devoted to the subject. The scientific method consists of a series of steps.

1. Come up with a **QUESTION** or try to solve a **PROBLEM**. What are you curious about?
2. **RESEARCH** your topic. Find out what is already known. Has anyone already answered your question or solved your problem? What facts are published about your topic?
3. Form a **HYPOTHESIS**, which is an answer to your question or a solution to your problem.
4. Design an **EXPERIMENT** to test your hypothesis. Collect and record the data from your experiment.
5. Study your experimental **RESULTS** and form a **CONCLUSION**. Was your hypothesis true or false?
6. **REPORT** your findings.

Symbols Used in This Book			
Cal	dietary calorie	lb	pound
g	gram	mL	milliliter
in	inch	mm	millimeter
L	liter	oz	ounce (can be used as measure of weight, where 16 oz = 1 lb, or volume as fluid ounce, where 33.8 oz = 1 L)

In writing formulas for compounds the following element symbols are used:

C	carbon	N	nitrogen
Ca	calcium	Na	sodium
Cl	chlorine	O	oxygen
H	hydrogen	P	phosphorus

Safety First

1. These experiments can be done in the kitchen at home or at school as part of a science class or lab. Make sure an adult in your household or teacher at your school knows what you are doing and has approved your activities. Ask a parent, teacher, or other adult if you need help with any experiment.

2. Clean up after each experiment is completed.

3. Follow any special instructions given in the experiment or given on the label of any product you are using.

4. Do not eat or drink while experimenting unless directed to do so as part of the activity.

Chapter 1

How Sweet It Is: Sugars and Sweeteners

What ingredient makes soda so sweet? All carbonated sodas have a sweet taste due to either natural sugars or artificial sweeteners. For example, a 12-oz (355-mL) can of cola may contain about 39 grams of sugar and have about 140 calories. A calorie is a measure of the energy content of food. A 12-oz can of diet cola may use an artificial sweetener such as aspartame in place of sugar. Because so little aspartame is used, a diet drink has approximately zero calories.

Natural sugars include fructose, glucose, lactose, and sucrose. These sugars are found in a variety of foods and in your body. Fructose is a sugar found in honey and fruit. Glucose is the type of sugar our bodies use for energy. Because glucose is found in blood, it is sometimes called blood sugar. Carbohydrates in food such as bread and pasta are broken down into glucose molecules as part of the digestion process. Lactose is the sugar found in milk. When someone says, "Pass the sugar," what he is really saying is "Pass the sucrose." Sucrose is the white sugar found in the sugar bowl. Each sucrose molecule is a combination of fructose and glucose linked together.

Regular (non-diet) sodas use either sucrose or fructose for sweetness. Corn syrup can be converted to fructose. Fructose made from corn syrup is cheaper than sucrose and can be sweeter.

Common artificial sweeteners include aspartame, acesulfame potassium, and saccharin. Saccharin is about 500 times sweeter than the same amount of sucrose. Saccharin was discovered by accident in 1879. It was produced for general use starting in 1900. The sweetness of aspartame was also discovered by chance in 1965. Aspartame is about 200 times sweeter than sucrose.

Diet Coke and many other diet sodas use aspartame for sweetness. Artificial sweeteners are much sweeter than the same amount of sucrose, so very little is needed to sweeten a drink. The body does not digest saccharin, so it has no calories. Aspartame is digested, but because such a tiny amount is used in a drink, there are almost no calories produced.

In the experiments in this chapter, you can detect the presence of sweetener or sugar in a soda by floating or sinking it. You can remove water by evaporation and observe the amount of sugar or sweetener in a drink. You can determine the amount of sugar by measuring relative density. You can also use food labels to count food energy in calories.

Experiment 1.1
Cola Float— Regular or Diet

In this experiment, you will explore the effects of sugar and trapped gas in making a can of soda float or sink. The object of this experiment and further investigation is to determine which cans of soda float or sink in water and why.

Materials

* large bucket
* water
* can of Coke
* can of diet Coke

Fill a large bucket with water. Make sure the water is about room temperature—not hot or cold. Place unopened cans of Coke and diet Coke into the water. They may be room temperature or cold. What happens? Can you explain your observations?

Density is a measure of mass or weight per volume. Suppose you have a fixed volume of liquid. As the density of the liquid increases, the same volume becomes heavier. In science, density is usually given as grams per milliliter (g/mL). At room temperature, water has a density of about 1.0 g/mL.

Ice cream includes tiny air bubbles that lower its density and give it a softer taste. The air is whipped into the cream as it is frozen. In an ice cream float, ice cream can float in liquid cola. The ice cream floats because it is less dense, or lighter, than the same volume of liquid cola. In this experiment, does the diet Coke float? Are the contents of the diet Coke less dense than water? Does the regular Coke sink? Is its density greater than water's density?

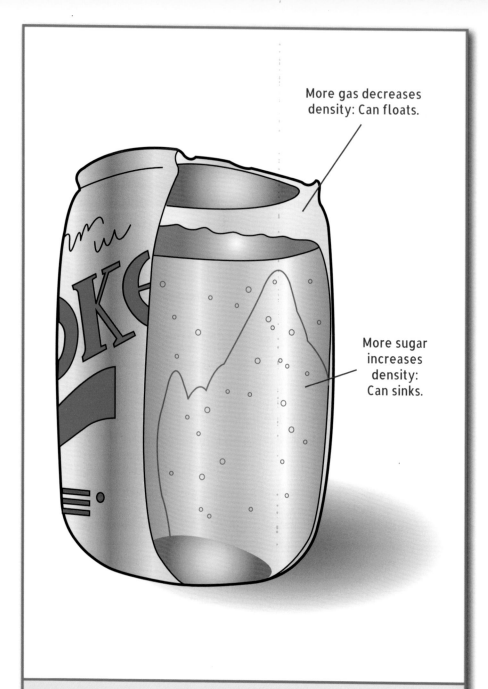

More gas decreases density: Can floats.

More sugar increases density: Can sinks.

Figure 1. When more sugar is added to a drink, the density is increased and the can is more likely to sink.

If you look on a can of cola, you may see that there are about 39 g of sugar. If 355 mL of cola contains 355 g of water plus 39 g of sugar, then the density can be approximated as 394 g divided by 355 mL, or about 1.1 g/mL. Since this added sugar causes the cola's density to be greater than the density of water, a can of regular cola should sink. In place of sugar, a diet cola has only a tiny amount of a sweetener—such as aspartame. Therefore a diet cola has a density close to the density of water.

If diet cola has the same density as water, why would it float? The diet drink floats because there is a pocket of carbon dioxide gas inside the can. The diet and regular colas both have the same amount of gas trapped inside their cans. This gas would make both cans float, but the regular one sinks because the sugar adds extra weight. The trapped carbon dioxide gas lowers the density inside the can. Including the gas and the liquid, the contents of a diet cola can are less dense than water. While adding sugar increases the density, the space filled with gas lowers the density inside the can (see Figure 1). If the pocket of gas were large enough, then even the regular cola would float.

A submarine is like a can of soda. To make a submarine go down, seawater replaces air in huge tanks to make the submarine heavier. To make the submarine go up, air is pumped back into the same containers. The air pushes out the water and makes the submarine lighter. If enough air is pumped into a submarine, it can float on the surface of the ocean.

Project Ideas and Further Investigations

- Make a table with three columns labeled Drink Name, Diet or Regular, and Float or Sink. Repeat this experiment with as many different types of cans of regular and diet carbonated soft drinks (Sprite, Pepsi, etc.) as you can locate. Record your observations.

- Do all sugar-containing drinks sink? Do all diet drinks float? Does using cans labeled *Caffeine* or *Caffeine-free* make any difference in the results?

LEFT BEHIND— EVAPORATION AND SUGAR CONTENT

The object of this experiment is to compare the rates of evaporation and amounts of material left after evaporation for three different soft drinks. In this work you are looking for any differences between regular (sugar-containing), diet, and caffeine-free diet drinks.

Materials
* permanent marker
* 3 clear disposable plastic cups
* liquid measuring cup
* cola
* diet cola
* caffeine-free diet cola
* ruler

Water is made of molecules. A molecule is a collection of atoms. A molecule of water can be written as H_2O, meaning that a water molecule has two hydrogen atoms and one oxygen atom. Have you ever seen a puddle of water gradually disappear on a hot summer day? What happened to the water?

Some molecules of water may have gained enough energy to leave the liquid state, become a gas, and go into the air. When molecules leave a liquid this way, it is called evaporation (it becomes a vapor). As evaporation continues, there are fewer liquid molecules and more gas or vapor molecules. On a hot sunny day, a puddle can disappear in a few hours. Higher temperatures make molecules move faster, or gives them energy. The molecules of H_2O are not destroyed, but they are changed from a liquid to a gas.

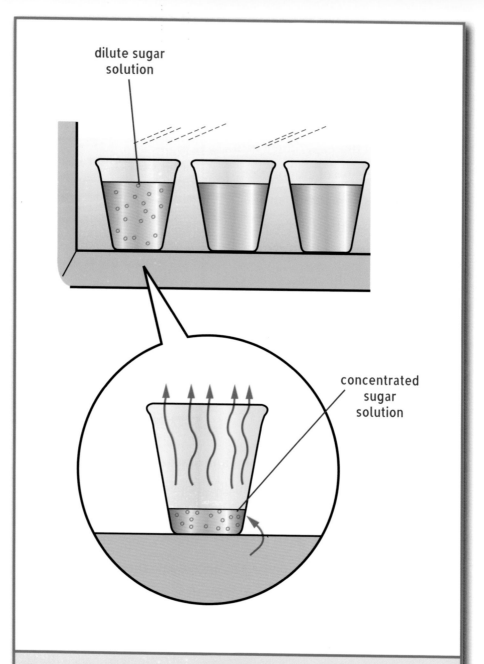

dilute sugar solution

concentrated sugar solution

Figure 2. As water evaporates, it leaves sugar and other dissolved molecules behind. A solution becomes more concentrated as water leaves and sugar remains behind.

When evaporation occurs, other things in the water such as salts, sugars, acids, additives, or coloring molecules do not go into the air. Only the water evaporates (see Figure 2). In many places around the world, table salt, NaCl, is produced by allowing salt water to evaporate from shallow ponds. The water leaves, but the salt remains behind. In this experiment, you will explore the evaporation of water from several different types of cola and observe what is left behind.

Use a permanent marker to label three clear disposable plastic cups *Regular Cola, Diet Cola,* and *Caffeine-free Diet Cola.* Add exactly one cup of regular cola, one cup of diet cola, and one cup of caffeine-free diet cola to the correct plastic cups. Use a ruler to measure the height (in millimeters) of the liquid in each cup. Make a table in your science notebook with columns for the date and height of each of the three liquids. Label the columns *Date, Height (mm) of Regular Cola, Height (mm) of Diet Cola*, and *Height (mm) of Caffeine-free Diet Cola*. Record the date and the heights of the three liquids. Set the cups in a place where they can remain undisturbed for several weeks, such as on a windowsill.

Observe the cups and measure the liquid levels every other day for the next several weeks. How quickly the water levels drop depends on the temperature in the room and if the cups are in direct sunlight or not. Continue observing the cups. After three to five weeks of evaporation, compare what remains in each of the three cups. If you still have liquid in any of the cups, continue the experiment.

After three weeks, what do you observe in each cup? Is there liquid left in the diet cups? Is there liquid left in the regular cup?

In diet drinks only a small amount of sweetener is needed to give the drink its sweet taste. Look on the labels for the regular and diet drinks and read the ingredients that are listed beyond carbonated water. These items may remain in the cups when the water is gone. Once the water molecules are gone, you may observe that the amounts of ingredients in both diet drinks are quite small. However, in the bottom of the cup of regular cola, you may find thick syrup (sugar and some water) remaining. There are many sugar molecules that cannot evaporate. They stay in the cup.

If a 12-oz can of regular cola contains about 39 g of sugar (see the label on the can), then one cup (8 oz) of cola should have about 26 g of sugar. If you drink 12 cans of cola you will consume over one pound of sugar, since 12 x 39 g = 468 g, and 1 lb = 454 g.

Project Ideas and Further Investigations

- Make a plot of the height data you collected for each drink. Plot the height of liquid versus the number of days of evaporation. Compare the shape of the curves made by each set of data points.
- Repeat this experiment and compare the rates of evaporation in a colder or warmer room or in a dark or sunny location.
- Add four drops of red food coloring to two cups of water. Mix well and then pour one cup of this red water into a clear plastic bottle. Screw the cap on the top of the bottle. Pour the other cup of red water into a clear disposable plastic cup. Set this cup where it will not be disturbed and check it once a week for the next four weeks. Does either liquid get darker each week? After four weeks compare the amount of liquid in the bottle and in the cup. Can you explain what happened?

Experiment 1.3
DETERMINING THE DENSITY OF COLA

In this activity you will observe which sugar-water mixtures float and which sink in cola. The object of this experiment is to determine the density of cola.

Density is a measure of mass divided by volume. (As sugar is added to water, density increases.) The density of a sugar-and-water mixture can be expressed as grams of sugar per ounce of liquid (g/oz). The ounces (oz) used in this experiment are fluid ounces. Fluid ounces are commonly used to measure volume of liquids. Look on a 2-liter drink bottle label and you should observe that this volume is about 68 fluid ounces.

Materials

* an adult
* plastic 2-liter bottle of cola
* pitcher
* scissors
* 6 plastic 8-oz water bottles with caps
* permanent marker
* funnel
* teaspoon
* sugar
* water
* tongs

Remove the label from a 2-liter clear plastic bottle of regular cola. Pour the cola from the bottle into a pitcher. **With an adult's help** cut off the cone-shaped top of the empty 2-liter bottle. Allow the cola in the pitcher to remain open to the air for several days until the cola goes flat, or loses its carbonation. Pour the flat cola back into the topless soda bottle.

Remove the labels from six clear 8-oz plastic bottles (the small size used for some bottled water). Make sure the bottles are empty and clean. Use a permanent marker to label each bottle as *0, 2, 4, 6, 8,* or *10.* Using a funnel, fill the bottles with 0, 2, 4, 6, 8, or 10 level teaspoons of sugar. Make sure each spoon contains an amount of sugar level with the top of the spoon—not rounded. Each spoonful of sugar should have the same volume.

Fill each bottle halfway with water and screw the caps on the bottles. Shake each bottle until its sugar is completely dissolved. Place the bottles on a flat surface. Fill each bottle with water until the water forms a curve above the mouth of the bottle. Carefully screw the cap on each bottle so that the bottles remain filled. Invert each bottle and observe if there is any air trapped inside. It is important that air not be left in the bottles.

Make a table (see Figure 3) with four columns labeled *Teaspoons of Sugar, Grams of Sugar, Grams of Sugar per Ounce,* and *Float or Sink.* Under the first column, write *0, 2, 4, 6, 8,* and *10.* Each teaspoon of sugar weighs about 5 grams. Multiply the teaspoons of sugar by 5 g to find the grams of sugar in each bottle. Record these calculations under Grams of Sugar. The 8-oz bottle when completely filled with water contains about 9 oz of water (because 8 ounces of water do not completely fill the bottle). Divide the grams of sugar in each bottle (0, 10, 20, 30, 40, and 50) by 9 oz. For example, 50 g divided by 9 oz = 5.6 g/oz. Record the results of these calculations under *Grams of Sugar per Ounce.* Now you are ready to make your observations.

Place the closed bottle labeled 0 into the cola. Wait a minute and observe whether the bottle floats or sinks (see Figure 4). Use tongs to remove the bottle from the cola. Repeat this activity with each of the other bottles. Record which bottles float and which sink.

Note that the mass of the plastic may slightly affect your results. Also, any air pocket left in the bottle will lower the density.

The concentration of fluid is a measure of the grams of sugar. The greater the concentration of sugar, the greater the density (mass per volume) of the liquid. All the bottles filled with sugar water that float must have a density less than the cola density. However, the bottles that sink must have a density greater than the cola. Using your observations, what do you estimate for the density of cola?

The label on a bottle of cola may report that it has about 26 g of sugar in 8 oz of liquid. Using the numbers from this labeled amount of sugar, you could calculate 26 g/8 oz = 3.3 g/oz. This sample calculation shows that in every one ounce of cola fluid there are about 3.3 grams of sugar. What density do you calculate for the cola? How does your experimental density compare to the density calculated from the label?

Density Determination Table			
Teaspoons of Sugar	Grams of Sugar	Grams of Sugar per Ounce	Float or Sink
0	0 g	0 g/oz	float
2	10 g	1.1 g/oz	---
4	20 g	2.2 g/oz	---
6	30 g	3.3 g/oz	---
8	40 g	4.4 g/oz	---
10	50 g	5.6 g/oz	---

Figure 3. Make a table with the columns shown. Record your density calculations, and note whether each bottle floats or sinks.

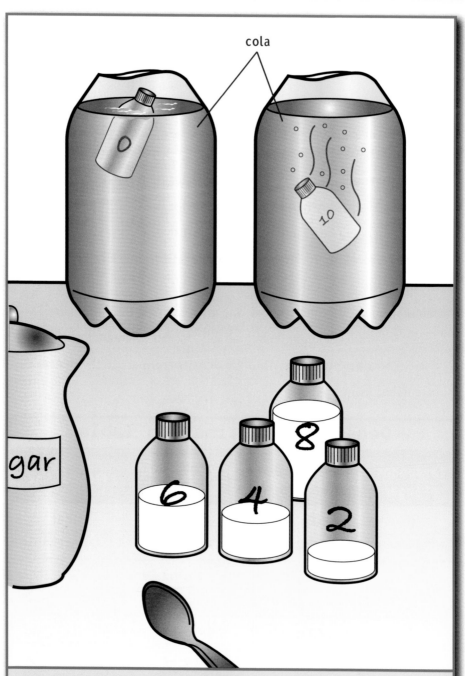

Figure 4. Bottles filled with sugar water float if their density is less than cola and sink if their density if greater than cola.

You can repeat this experiment and get more accurate results by measuring exactly the amount of water required to completely fill the small bottles you used. If this number is different than 9 oz, you can redo your data table calculations of g/oz. Divide the grams of sugar in each bottle (0, 10, 20, 30, 40, and 50) by the corrected number of fluid ounces. Then correct the rest of the table.

Project Idea and Further Investigation

There is another way to determine the amount of sugar in water. You can find the minimum amount of air required to float an 8-oz plastic bottle containing regular cola in a sink filled with water. Begin with the bottle completely filled with cola. This bottle should sink. Pour out a teaspoon of cola and test the bottle to see if it floats. Continue removing and testing the bottle until it is just light enough to float in the water. Remember: Adding air lowers the density and adding sugar increases the density.

Now fill another 8-oz bottle with water to the same level as you now have in the cola bottle. This bottle should float. Add a teaspoon of sugar to this water bottle and test for floating. Continue adding sugar and testing until it is just heavy enough to sink. The amount of sugar you added to the water bottle should be about the same as the amount of sugar in cola. Compare your result to the amount of sugar listed on the bottle.

Experiment 1.4

CALCULATING CALORIES

If you are interested in what you eat, it would be great to have a special lab where careful measurements could be made to determine the number of calories in each kind of food. It would also be important to be able to measure the fat, carbohydrates, and protein in your food. Fortunately, we do not need a special lab because food companies have already done these analyses.

Materials

* food containers or packages for ginger ale, cola, milk, turkey, ham, cheese, ice cream, bologna, and at least four other foods
* calculator

They are required by law to reveal all their results on their labels. The object of this experiment is to find if you can use food labels to calculate the number of calories found in each gram of fat, carbohydrate, and protein.

Gather at least 12 different food containers or packages as indicated in the materials list. Find the Nutrition Facts label on each food. In your science notebook, set up a chart to record your data (see Figure 5). Use the Nutrition Facts serving size numbers to record the calories, calories from fat, total fat, total carbohydrates (carbs), and total protein. The total calories per serving and calories from fat per serving are based on the serving size shown on the package. The total fat, carbohydrates, or protein is measured in grams (454 g = 1 lb).

The first step is to calculate the calories per gram of fat. For each food that has at least 3 grams fat, divide the calories from fat by the total grams of fat. Record all the numbers from these calculations. When you are finished, find the average of these numbers and round off to the nearest whole number. You should now have the number of calories per gram of fat.

The second step is to calculate the calories per gram of carbohydrate. For ginger ale and cola there are no grams of fat and no grams of protein. All the calories come from carbohydrates (sugar is a type of carbohydrate). For both cola and ginger ale, divide the listed calories by the total grams of carbohydrates. If you have any other foods that are only carbohydrates, then include these in this calculation. Find the average of these numbers and round off to the nearest whole number. You should now have the number of calories per gram of carbohydrate.

Nutrition Facts for Servings of Different Foods

Food	Calories	Calories from Fat	Fat, grams	Carbohydrate, grams	Protein, grams
Cola	140	0	0	39	0
Snack Mix	160	80	9	18	4
Milk					

Figure 5. Prepare a table of nutrition facts for at least 12 different foods. These numbers will be used for your food energy calculations of calories per gram for fat, carbohydrate, and protein.

The third step is to calculate the calories per gram of protein. You will do these calculations only for foods that have at least 6 grams of protein per serving. For each food selected, you will need to first get the carbohydrate calories by multiplying the calories per gram of carbohydrate times the grams of carbohydrate. The fat calories are listed on the label, so you do not have to calculate them. Find the protein calories by the following calculation:

$$\text{Protein Calories} = \text{Total Calories} - \text{Fat Calories} - \text{Carbohydrate Calories}$$

Finally, divide the protein calories by the grams of protein in each food.

When you are finished, find the average of these numbers and round off to the nearest whole number. You should now have a number of calories per gram of protein.

Compare your results to the values that scientists use of 9 calories per gram of fat, 4 calories per gram of carbohydrate, and 4 calories per gram of protein. How close are the values that you found for fat, carbohydrate, and protein to the values that scientists use?

Project Ideas and Further Investigations

- Repeat the calculations in this experiment with additional foods and see if the results change. In science it is important to include enough measurements or numbers to be able to get a reliable average.
- Use the calorie-per-gram numbers of 9 for fat, 4 for protein, and 4 for carbohydrate and the listed grams of fat, protein, and carbohydrate per serving on a food label to calculate the total

number of calories per serving, as shown below. The protein calories are equal to the listed grams of protein times the value of 4 Cal/g. The fat and carbohydrate calories are calculated in a similar way. If there were a food with 10 g of protein, 6 g of fat, and 30 g of carbohydrate per serving, then the calculation would be done as shown below.

$$\frac{\text{Total}}{\text{Calories}} = \frac{\text{Protein}}{\text{Calories}} + \frac{\text{Fat}}{\text{Calories}} + \frac{\text{Carbohydrate}}{\text{Calories}}$$

$$\frac{\text{Total}}{\text{Calories}} = 10\,g \times \frac{4\,\text{Cal}}{g} + 6\,g \times \frac{9\,\text{Cal}}{g} + 30\,g \times \frac{4\,\text{Cal}}{g}$$

$$\frac{\text{Total}}{\text{Calories}} = 214\,\text{Cal}$$

Compare your answer to the total calories listed per serving on the label. Repeat this calculation for as many different foods as possible. Make a table listing each food, its serving size, the reported calories per serving, and your calculated calories per serving. How close are your calculated total calories to the listed total calories?

Chapter 2

FIZZY DRINKS: CARBON DIOXIDE IN ACTION

Do you like the fizzy sensation in your mouth when you take a sip of your favorite soft drink? Some people like it and some people don't. What makes this fizz? If you look on a can or bottle of any carbonated drink, the first ingredient listed is carbonated water. Carbonated water is water that contains dissolved carbon dioxide (CO_2). The trapped CO_2 gas causes bubbles to form when a bottle is opened. Dissolved CO_2 also gives water a taste that is sometimes described as "sharp" or "acidic." Flavored carbonated beverages are called soda or soda pop because an early method of making the CO_2 involved reacting carbonate of soda (Na_2CO_3, also called sodium carbonate) or bicarbonate of soda ($NaHCO_3$, also called sodium bicarbonate, or baking soda) with acid. Carbonated water is sometimes called seltzer water.

Carbon dioxide gas makes up about 0.04 percent of the earth's atmosphere. This gas has no odor and no color and will not burn. If the pressure is increased to 50 times the normal pressure of our atmosphere, then gaseous CO_2 will change to liquid. Liquid CO_2 can be stored in steel tanks and in this form is used by bottling companies.

Solubility is a measure of the ability of a substance to dissolve or go into a liquid. More CO_2 gas will dissolve in water as the water becomes colder. Carbon dioxide also dissolves more readily (becomes more soluble) as the pressure of the carbon dioxide gas above the water is higher. In 1803 William Henry showed that the solubility of gas becomes greater as the pressure of the gas is increased. This general principle later came to be called Henry's law. Because of these temperature and pressure effects, carbonated water is made and bottled using high-pressure carbon dioxide and cold water. The pressure at which some carbonated beverages are sealed is about three times the normal pressure of the atmosphere. The volume of CO_2 gas when released from the carbonated liquid may be two to five times the volume of the liquid.

Naturally occurring carbonated mineral waters were known in ancient times and considered to be of medical benefit. Flemish chemist Jan Baptista Van Helmont (1579–1644) discovered carbon dioxide. Joseph Priestley, a famous English chemist who later moved to America, found in 1767 that CO_2 dissolved in water gave it an "acidulated" taste that people enjoyed. William Brownrigg, an English physician, presented a paper before the Royal Society (a British scientific society) in 1765 about the pleasant taste that CO_2 gave water.

In America, the first carbonated waters were manufactured in 1785. Many countries around the world developed a carbonated water industry. By 1835 there were 64 carbonated water bottling facilities in the United States. By 1875 this number had increased to 512. By 1957 there were 5,200 bottling facilities for carbonated beverages, just in America.

As flavors were added to carbonated water, the drinks became more popular and the soft drink industry grew rapidly. The industry also developed because of technological advancements: Improvements in the production of liquid CO_2 allowed bottlers to buy it in tanks instead of making it themselves. The crown cap invented by William Painter in 1892 provided a reliable method to seal glass bottles. Machine-made bottles allowed all bottles to be exactly the same, so machines could be developed for cleaning, filling, and capping the identical bottles.

Commercial bottlers normally get syrup flavors from another company. They use liquid CO_2 stored in metal tanks. They add this CO_2 to chilled water to make carbonated water. They place the syrup in a can or bottle, add the carbonated water, and seal the container. When you get a carbonated drink at a fast-food restaurant and fill your cup, you are doing something like what the bottlers do. When you press a button, CO_2 is mixed with water and syrup on its way to your cup.

In this chapter you will explore many fascinating properties of CO_2 gas and the foam that it creates. You will examine the effects of temperature and pressure, measure amounts dissolved, and study fizzy foam lifetimes.

Experiment 2.1

TRAPPING CARBON DIOXIDE

In this simple experiment, you will capture all the carbon dioxide gas that escapes from a carbonated beverage after it is opened. The object of this experiment is to measure the amount of gas released from a carbonated soda and compare it to the amount of starting liquid.

Place an unopened 500-mL bottle of cola inside a large resealable bag. Press down to seal the plastic bag, but leave a small opening in the corner. Now, push down on the bag to remove as much air as possible from inside the bag. You want the bag to be flat except where it surrounds the bottle. After you have flattened the bag, seal the bag completely.

Hold the bottle through the bag and carefully twist the cap. Holding the cap through the bag, twist a little at a time until the cap is completely removed. Tilt the bottle and bag to pour all the liquid out of the bottle and into the sealed bag.

Observe the bag for a few minutes. What do you see? Holding the bag over a sink, shake the bag a few times and then set it down.

Let the bag sit undisturbed in the sink for one hour and then check it again. Does the bag contain more liquid or more gas?

Materials

* plastic 0.5-liter (500-mL) bottle of cola
* one-gallon resealable bag
* sink
* permanent marker
* measuring container marked in milliliters

There are 500 mL of liquid in the bag. Can you guess how much gas is in the bag?

Here is a method that you can use to measure the amount of gas trapped in the bag. Roll one side of the gas-filled bag as far as it will go until it is tight. Mark a line on the bag with a permanent marker at the place where the bag is rolled (see Figure 6). Open the bag, and remove the empty bottle and cap but leave the liquid cola in the bag. Keeping careful track of the total amount of water, add water from a measuring container until the bag is filled up to your mark. The volume of water that you added to reach the mark is the same as the volume of gas that was trapped inside the bag.

Although the bag contained only half a liter of liquid, you may find that the bag contained two or more liters of gas. How could so much gas come from so little liquid?

In a closed soda bottle, water molecules surround molecules of carbon dioxide. Some carbon dioxide also combines with water to make carbonic acid. When you open a soft drink bottle, carbon dioxide gas that is dissolved into the water of the cola bubbles out of the liquid. Molecules in a liquid are close together, but molecules in a gas are far apart. As the carbon dioxide gas leaves the liquid, it fills the empty bag. A small volume of carbon dioxide dissolved in the liquid can fill a much larger volume as free gas. Most of the volume occupied by a gas is actually empty space between the moving molecules.

Project Ideas and Further Investigations

- Repeat this experiment with as many different brands of carbonated sodas as you can locate. Make a table with four columns labeled *Drink Name, Volume of Liquid, Volume of*

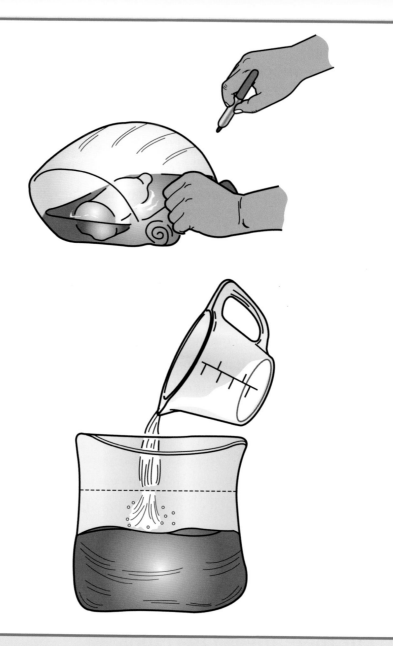

Figure 6. Roll one side of the gas-filled bag until it is tight. Mark a line on the sealed bag with a permanent marker at the place where the bag is rolled. You will be able to use this mark to determine how much carbon dioxide gas is trapped in the bag.

Gas, and *Ratio of Gas Volume to Liquid.* In the first column of the table, list the name of the drink. In the second column, list the volume in milliliters of the drink. The volume of liquid in the bottle is usually given in both oz and mL. In the third column, record the volume (mL) of gas that you measure. To find the ratio of gas volume to liquid, divide the number in column three by the number in column two. This division gives you the ratio of milliliters of gas per milliliter of liquid. This ratio allows you to compare drinks that may come in different sized bottles.

- You may be able to repeat the above experiment using different carbonated drinks that come in cans. However, you will have to be careful not to tear the bag as you open the can. Try as many different drinks as you can to compare the amount of carbonation. You can compare amounts of gas found in plastic bottles and aluminum cans for the same drink.

TEMPERATURE AND GOING FLAT

Have you had a carbonated beverage that has gone flat, or lost its fizz? In this experiment you will explore the role of temperature in keeping a cola from going flat and losing its dissolved carbon dioxide gas.

Leave one unopened bottle of cola in a refrigerator overnight, and leave an identical unopened bottle of cola out at room temperature. The next day fill a plastic bowl with ice. Run the sink water on the hot setting for several minutes. Fill another plastic bowl with hot tap water about 13 cm (5 in) deep. Remove the bottle from the refrigerator.

Materials

* 2 identical plastic bottles of cola, unopened
* refrigerator
* 2 large plastic bowls
* ice
* sink with hot and cold water
* partner
* 2 balloons
* clock or watch with second hand

Have a partner help you with the next part so that you can start both bottles at the same time. Gently unscrew the caps on both bottles. Quickly place balloons over the top of each bottle. After each balloon is securely in place, shake the bottles up and down about three times. Place the cold bottle in the ice-filled bowl. Place the room-temperature bottle in the hot water (see Figure 7).

Compare the size of the two balloons each minute for the next six minutes. Carbon dioxide gas will gradually pass through the rubber balloon, so the balloons will not stay inflated permanently.

Figure 7. Place a cold bottle of cola in ice and a room-temperature bottle of cola in hot water and observe how quickly the balloons inflate.

The balloons get bigger as carbon dioxide molecules leave the liquid. As soon as you open a sealed bottle, the pressure decreases above the liquid and carbon dioxide leaves as a gas. How rapidly this happens depends on the pressure above the liquid and the temperature of the liquid. In your experiment, does cold cola or warm cola release more gas?

Project Idea and Further Investigation

Use a permanent marker to mark the level of the liquid in an unopened cola bottle. Open the bottle and quickly place a balloon over the bottle. While holding the balloon on the bottle, turn the bottle upside down. Then return it to an upright position. Shake the bottle occasionally. When the balloon stops getting larger, once again mark the level of the liquid in the bottle. How does the volume of the liquid decrease compare to the increase in the size of the balloon? Repeat this experiment for different carbonated drinks and compare.

Experiment 2.3
PUSH OF PRESSURE

The object of this experiment is to determine how the pressure on a liquid affects the release of dissolved carbon dioxide gas from that liquid. You will explore the balance between dissolved and gaseous carbon dioxide.

Materials

* unopened bottle of Sprite (16- or 20-oz size)

Remove the label from an unopened plastic bottle of Sprite. Place the bottle on a table and look at the clear liquid. Do you see any bubbles? Unscrew the cap slightly and listen for the sound of gas escaping from the bottle. Watch the liquid as you unscrew the cap. What do you see? As soon as you see bubbles rising, screw the cap back on tight. Shake the bottle twice and set it back on the table. Look closely at the liquid.

Once again do these steps: Open the cap slightly while watching the liquid, tightly close the cap, shake the bottle twice, and set the bottle on the table. Repeat these steps several times. Record your observations.

You probably see bubbles forming and rising in the bottle whenever the cap is opened. When the cap is opened, the pressure is decreased and carbon dioxide gas escapes from the liquid. As the pressure drops, bubbles form and rise in the liquid. This gas escapes into the surrounding air. When the cap is closed and you shake the bottle, it causes more gas to bubble up. However, this gas is trapped inside the bottle, and it increases the pressure. This increase in

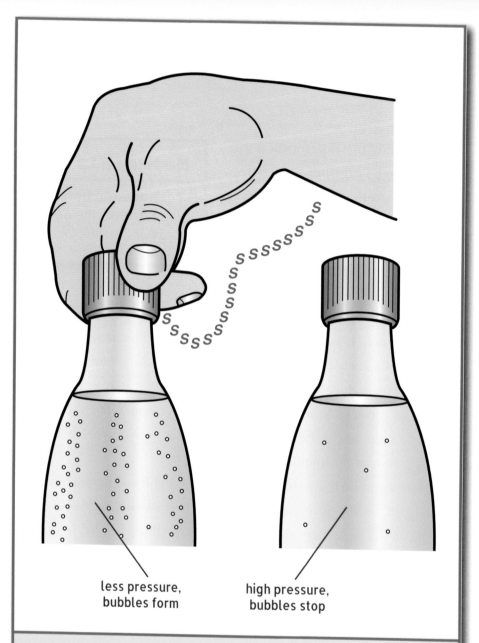

less pressure, bubbles form

high pressure, bubbles stop

Figure 8. In an opened bottle, the pressure drops and carbon dioxide gas escapes, causing bubbles to rise in the liquid. In a closed bottle, gas is trapped inside the bottle, the pressure increases, and bubbles stop forming.

pressure inside the bottle stops more gas from leaving the liquid (see Figure 8).

Carbon dioxide, CO_2, dissolved in water makes the water acidic. This is because the CO_2 combines with the water, H_2O, to form carbonic acid, H_2CO_3. There is a balance in water between the dissolved CO_2 molecules and the carbonic acid molecules. We exhale CO_2 and our bodies use this carbon dioxide gas and carbonic acid system to help control blood acidity.

The balance between oxygen and carbon dioxide gases found in our lungs and dissolved in blood is important in medicine and understanding certain diseases of the lungs. For example, people with chronic obstructive pulmonary disease (COPD) cannot effectively exhale carbon dioxide because of damage to their lungs. As a result, too much carbon dioxide gas builds up in their bloodstream, and their blood becomes too acidic. The blood eventually cannot deliver enough oxygen to the body, which can be fatal.

The balance between dissolved and free gas is also important in scuba diving. At increasing underwater depths, divers experience greater pressure from the water around them because there is more water stacked above them. At these higher pressures, nitrogen gas dissolves in blood and joints.

When divers that have been in deep water rise to the surface, nitrogen that was dissolved in their blood and joints bubbles out. If they rise suddenly to the surface, gas will bubble out just like when a soft drink bottle is opened. This escaping gas causes painful cramps called the "bends" and a dangerous medical condition known as decompression sickness. Divers can avoid these ailments by rising slowly to the surface so that the dissolved gas can escape gradually.

Project Idea and Further Investigation

Open a clear carbonated soda and pour it into a glass. Drop two grapes and two raisins into the soda and watch them for several minutes. What do you observe? Bubbles of carbon dioxide can attach to solid objects and lower their density. When the density is lowered, the objects rise in the liquid. When the bubbles break at the surface, the object may rotate around the surface and then sink, or just sink directly. Try different carbonated sodas and seltzer waters and measure the total time that raisins or grapes will rise and fall. For different drinks, is this time longer if there is more dissolved carbon dioxide originally in the liquid? See Experiment 2.1 to help you develop a new experiment to test this hypothesis.

Fizzy Foam Lifetime

Have you ever poured soda into a glass and watched foam form and then disappear? Did you know that ice cream is a type of frozen foam? Ice cream contains ice crystals; liquid water with dissolved sugars, salts, and proteins; and foam made of trapped air bubbles. The frozen foam of trapped air bubbles makes the ice cream soft and fluffy. The object of this activity is to measure the lifetime of foam under different conditions and determine how you can lengthen this lifetime.

Materials

* unopened bottle of cola
* liquid measuring cup
* tall, clear drinking glass
* watch or clock with a second hand
* sink
* milk (Keep in refrigerator until ready to use.)

Open a bottle of cola and gently pour 1/2 cup into a liquid measuring cup. Next, rapidly pour this cola into an empty drinking glass. You should see foam forming as soon as you pour the cola into the glass. Trapped bubbles of carbon dioxide gas escape from the soda when it is poured and create the foam. The foam may not last long because the bubbles break and the carbon dioxide gas goes into the air. Use a watch or clock with a second hand to measure exactly how long the foam remains on top of the liquid before it disappears. Start measuring the time as soon as you dump the soda into the glass.

Pour all the liquid out of the glass into the sink, and rinse the glass with water. Now add 1/2 cup of cold milk to the empty glass. Rinse the measuring cup with water. As you did previously, gently pour 1/2 cup of cola into the measuring cup. Next, rapidly pour this cola into the drinking glass holding the milk. Time how long the foam remains on the top of the liquid before it disappears.

Repeat the above step using 1/4 cup of milk and 1/2 cup of cola. Repeat again using 1/8 cup of milk and 1/2 cup of cola. Rinse and dry the glass and measuring cup after each experiment. For every new milk and cola combination, time how long the foam lasts. When you do the 1/8 cup milk and 1/2 cup cola combination, look carefully at the foam through the side of the glass. Does the collection of larger bubbles, with each bubble surrounded by others, look somewhat like a bee honeycomb? Watch it for several minutes. Describe what you see and how it changes with time.

In your science notebook, make a table that indicates the amount of milk, amount of cola, and the lifetime of the foam (see Figure 9). Repeat all the cola and milk combinations several times. Find the average foam lifetimes for each different combination.

Milk is a complex mixture that contains mostly water along with sugar, proteins, and fat. There are also salts and vitamins present in milk. The amount of fat in milk can vary, but it is listed on the milk carton as 1 percent, 2 percent, 4 percent, etc.

When a carbonated soda is poured into milk, the protein molecules and fat globules in the milk surround the carbon dioxide gas bubbles. The proteins and fat form a thin film that makes the walls of the foam. The film holds the carbon dioxide gas trapped and provides the structure of the foam. As time passes, the smaller bubbles break and form larger bubbles. Larger bubbles have less pressure inside and are more stable than the small ones. Gradually the larger bubbles also break and the foam disappears.

Bubbles don't last long with just pure cola because it lacks the supporting protein and fat molecules. As you add some milk, the foam should last longer. However, if you add too much milk, the foam lifetime gets shorter. Why? Colder milk also helps to support the fat-filled foam.

Proteins from barley help maintain the head (foamy top) on poured beer. The proteins create a network around the bubbles and help them last longer. Beer contains carbon dioxide gas that makes it fizz. Some beers have nitrogen gas added to help make more foam.

Amount of Milk	Amount of Cola	Lifetime of Foam	Average Lifetime of Foam
0	1/2 cup	trial 1: trial 2: trial 3:	
1/2 cup	1/2 cup	trial 1: trial 2: trial 3:	
1/4 cup	1/2 cup	trial 1: trial 2: trial 3:	
1/8 cup	1/2 cup	trial 1: trial 2: trial 3:	

Figure 9. Make a table, like the one shown here, to record the amounts of milk and cola, as well as the life of the foam

Have you seen the foam on ocean waves as they come on shore? Proteins coming from seaweed in the ocean help to provide the walls of this air-filled foam.

Project Ideas and Further Investigations

- Repeat this experiment with different amounts of cola and milk until you find the combination that gives the longest lasting foam. Explore the difference between using cold milk or warm milk.
- Repeat the experiment using different samples of milk containing various percentages of fat, such as 1 percent, 2 percent, and 4 percent. Does changing the amount of fat change the foam lifetime? Does changing the amount of fat in the milk affect the amount of milk that gives the longest lasting foam?

Chapter 3

SODA SCIENCE: ACIDS, ADDITIVES, AND ADHESIVES

Just like all other packaged products, cola has a list of ingredients. If you read the label on a can or bottle of cola, you should see that it contains carbonated water, high fructose corn syrup and/or sugar, caramel color, phosphoric acid and/or citric acid, natural flavors, and caffeine. Carbonated water is water that has had carbon dioxide forced into it at higher pressure (see Chapter 2). High fructose corn syrup and sucrose are types of sugars used to sweeten soda drinks (see Chapter 1). The properties of other common ingredients in colas are examined in this chapter.

An additive is something that is added to another thing. In drinks, additives may be used for color, sweetness, or flavor, or to maintain freshness and avoid spoiling. Potassium benzoate is used in some diet drinks as a preservative.

Caffeine is a natural ingredient found in coffee, tea, and Kola nuts. Caffeine ($C_8H_{10}N_4O_2$) acts as a stimulant. A similar compound named theobromine ($C_7H_8N_4O_2$) is found in chocolate.

The third ingredient listed after the carbonated water and sugar is caramel color. Caramel is used to provide the dark rich color found in colas. In one experiment in this chapter, you will try to remove caramel coloring from a soft drink.

Soft drinks frequently contain either phosphoric acid or citric acid. Phosphoric acid is common in cola drinks. Citric acid is common in clear drinks but also may be found in root beer and grape soda. In one experiment you will use an indicator to try to detect the presence of acid in clear carbonated drinks.

The third experiment in this chapter explores a surprising property of sugar-containing soft drinks. By heating cola to get rid of most of the water, sticky syrup is formed. This hot, sticky liquid can be used to make glue or adhesive.

ACIDIC OR BASIC DRINK

An acid is a substance that produces H_3O^+ ions in water. A base is a substance that produces OH^- ions in water. Ions are molecules that have a positive or negative electrical charge. If water contains more H_3O^+ than OH^-, then it is acidic. If it contains more OH^- than H_3O^+, then it is basic. If it contains equal amounts of H_3O^+ and OH^-, then it is neutral. In this experiment, you will use an indicator liquid made from red cabbage to find out if Sprite is acidic, basic, or neutral.

Tear red cabbage leaves into quarter-sized pieces. Place 2 cups of cabbage pieces into a cooking pan. Add 4 cups of water to the pan and cover the pan. **Have an adult** heat the pan on the stove until the liquid is gently boiling. Gently boil for about eight minutes, then turn off the heat and allow the liquid to cool for about 20 minutes. An odor from the cooked cabbage is normal.

Materials

* an adult
* red cabbage
* measuring cup
* pan with lid
* water
* stove
* kitchen timer or clock or watch
* funnel
* 2 empty (16- or 20-oz) plastic drink bottles
* 4 clear drinking glasses
* 4 pieces of white paper
* baking soda
* vinegar
* lemon-lime soda

Pour the cooled cabbage liquid through a funnel into two empty plastic drink bottles (16- or 20-oz). Screw the tops on the bottles and save the cabbage juice (cabbage-colored water) until you are ready to use it. Examine the boiled cabbage leaves. Has their color changed?

An indicator molecule can be a different color depending on whether it is in acidic or basic liquid. Almost all fruits and vegetables, including red cabbage, contain natural indicators that will dissolve in water and can change color. You will use a known acid and base to test the indicator liquid, and then use this indictor to test lemon-lime soda.

Place four clear drinking glasses on sheets of white paper (see Figure 10). Add 1/4 cup of cabbage juice to each of the glasses. What color is the liquid in the glasses?

Baking soda is a base called sodium bicarbonate ($NaHCO_3$). Add a pinch (small amount held between thumb and finger) of baking soda to the first glass. If the liquid is not blue, add more baking soda until the liquid turns blue. Add 1/4 cup of water to this glass.

Vinegar is a dilute solution of acetic acid ($C_2H_4O_2$) in water. Add 1/4 cup of vinegar to the second glass. Does the vinegar turn the liquid pink or red?

If the third glass is not purple, add small amounts of liquid from the first or second glass and adjust the acidity until you get a purple color. Then add 1/4 cup of water to this glass.

Red cabbage indicator molecules can go through several color changes depending on the water acidity. Water containing red cabbage indicator molecules will be green if very basic, blue if slightly basic to neutral, purple if neutral to slightly acidic, pink if more acidic, and red if very acidic. Does this summary agree with your observations?

1. BASE

¼ cup cabbage juice
pinch of baking soda
¼ cub water

2. ACID

¼ cup cabbage juice
¼ cub vinegar

3. NEUTRAL

¼ cup cabbage juice
¼ cub water

4. LEMON-LIME SODA

¼ cup cabbage juice
¼ cub lemon-lime soda

Figure 10. Set up the experiment using four clear drinking glasses, each on a sheet of white paper. Make three indicator solutions: (1) base, (2) acid, and (3) neutral. Add lemon-lime soda to the cabbage juice in glass 4. Is lemon-lime soda a base, an acid, or neutral?

Add 1/4 cup of lemon-lime soda to the fourth glass. What color does the soda produce—pink, purple, or blue? Is it an acidic or basic drink? Read the ingredients on the soda label. Do you find any acids or bases listed that could explain your observation?

Project Ideas and Further Investigations

- Repeat this experiment with other types of clear carbonated sodas. What do you observe? Clear sodas usually contain citric acid ($C_6H_8O_7$). Dark colas usually contain phosphoric acid (H_3PO_4). Some sodas contain both citric and phosphoric acids. Dissolved carbon dioxide by itself combines with water to some extent to form an acid called carbonic acid (H_2CO_3).
- Try other drinks like orange juice, lemon juice, cola, and milk and record the color changes you observe. In dark-colored liquids, you may still be able to use the cabbage juice. However, you will first need to dilute the liquid with water so that you can see through it. What color changes are you able to observe with cola and with other liquids? Are the drinks you tested acidic, basic, or neutral? Prepare a summary of all the drinks you tested.

REMOVING COLOR

In this experiment, you will use activated carbon to try to remove the color from a diet cola and from a grape soda. Activated carbon is a special type of black carbon pellet that is commonly used to remove impurities from aquarium water and from drinking water.

Using a funnel, add enough carbon pellets to two clear, clean plastic bottles to make a layer of pellets about 7.5 cm (3 in) deep in each bottle. Add 2 cups of water to each bottle to rinse the activated carbon solid. You may see bubbles rising from the carbon. Leave the water on the carbon for about five minutes and then pour out the water without losing the pellets. Again

Materials

* funnel
* 4 clear plastic bottles (16-oz size)
* activated carbon pellets (sold with fish aquarium supplies) (Dispose of the carbon pellets in the trash when the experiment is completed.)
* ruler
* measuring cup
* water
* clock or watch
* diet cola
* grape soda

add 2 cups of water to each bottle and let them sit for about five minutes. Carefully pour off all this water, but again be careful to not pour out any of the pellets. Do not pour the pellets into a sink because they may clog the drain.

Add enough diet cola to one bottle to cover the pellets, then add about 5 cm (2 in) more liquid above the top of the pellets.

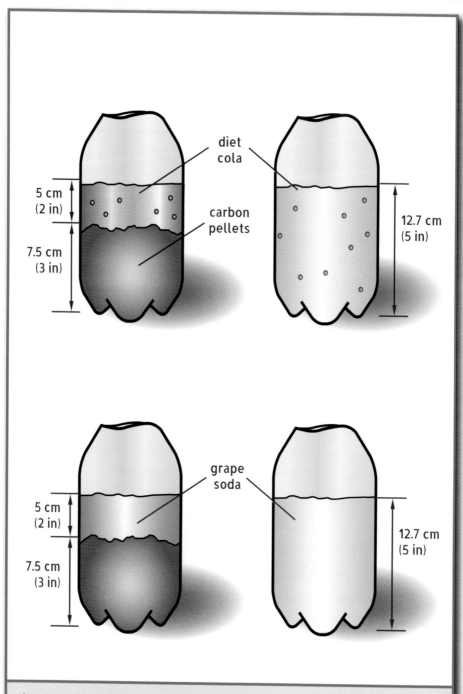

Figure 11. Set up your experiment using four clear plastic bottles.

Pour diet cola into an empty, pellet-free bottle until the liquid is the same height as in the pellet bottle. Pour enough grape soda to cover the pellets in a third bottle, then add about 5 cm (2 in) more liquid above the top of the pellets. Pour grape soda into an empty, pellet-free bottle until it is the same height. Screw a top on each of the four bottles (see Figure 11).

Observe each of the bottles and record a description in your science notebook of the color and darkness of the liquids. Can you see through the liquids? Are the liquids colorless or colored? Set the four bottles where they will not be disturbed for several days. Each day look at the liquids in the bottles and record your observations. Repeat your observations each day for a total of four days.

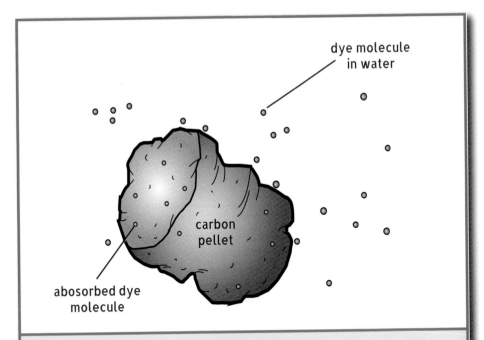

Figure 12. Molecules such as those responsible for color can be removed from water because they stick on the surface of carbon particles. This process is called adsorption and can be used to purify water.

What did you observe? Were there differences between the cola and grape soda? Explain your results.

If you look on the labels of cola drinks, you will see caramel color listed as one of the ingredients. Caramel coloring gives colas their characteristic rich, dark color. Caramel is made from heating sugar molecules. The longer it is heated, the darker the color formed. When heated to a golden brown, caramel can be used for flavoring. Caramel is also widely used to color other foods, such as soups, gravies, syrups, and puddings. In contrast, grape sodas often use a mixture of red and blue dye molecules (artificial food coloring) to produce their dark purple color.

Activated carbon has many cracks and crevices that give it a large surface area. This large surface area provides many places where molecules can stick. When an organic (carbon-containing) molecule such as a dye molecule is removed from water to stick on a solid surface, it is adsorbed (see Figure 12). Filters containing activated carbon are used to adsorb undesirable molecules. These carbon filters can purify drinking water and water in fish aquariums.

Project Idea and Further Investigation

Repeat this experiment with other types of colored liquids such as coffee, tea, orange juice, sport drinks, or other soft drinks. If the drink is a very dark color, you may need to dilute it with water. Make a table with the name of each type of drink and how it looks each day for four days with activated carbon pellets. What drinks lose their color the fastest? What drinks lose the most color?

Experiment 3.3
A Sticky Solution— Making Glue

Throughout history, glue has been made from natural products such as eggs, flour, or animal blood, or from boiling animal hoofs or bones to make a sticky gelatin. However, since World War II many synthetic (human-made) adhesives have been created.

You have probably used glue many times. However, in this experiment you will use cola to make your own glue.

Place a disposable aluminum pie pan on a metal baking tray. Pour a can of cola into the pie pan. **With an adult's help**, place the tray into an oven and set the oven at 400°F. Open the oven about every 15 minutes to observe how much liquid is left in the pie pan. The water in the cola will gradually evaporate (leave as gas molecules). You may have to heat the liquid for an hour or two to evaporate most of the water.

When almost all the water is gone, you should observe a sticky, dark, bubbling liquid in the bottom of the pie pan. This should be a viscous (thick and slow-pouring) liquid. When the liquid has

Materials

* an adult
* disposable aluminum pie pan
* metal baking tray
* can of cola
* oven
* watch or timer
* oven mitts
* 2 empty aluminum soda cans
* 2 small pieces of wood
* 2 disposable plastic spoons
* tongs

reached this condition, **ask an adult** to use oven mitts to remove the baking tray from the oven and place it on the stovetop.

You will need to use this glue while it is still hot, so you will need to work quickly. **Do not touch the hot liquid. Ask an adult** to use tongs to hold the top of an empty aluminum soda can and press the bottom of the can into the dark cola-glue. Then press this can down onto the top of another empty can. Hold the cans pressed together for about 20 seconds. Then set the cans aside and let the adhesive cool. If you push the pieces firmly together and leave a weight on top while they cool, you should get an even better seal.

Ask an adult to wipe a piece of wood across the hot sticky liquid and then press this wood onto another piece of wood. Press the pieces together and hold for 20 seconds. Set the wood pieces aside to cool.

Finally, **ask an adult** to spread the hot cola-glue into a plastic spoon and stick another spoon on top. Press together. Let the spoons cool.

Wait about 20 minutes and then test the metal cans, wood pieces, and plastic spoons. Can you pull the pairs of items apart? Did the cola make good glue? In very strong glues, one solid will break before the layer of glue will allow the two original solids to separate from each other.

Glue is a type of adhesive. Adhesives may hold two solids together by chemical bonding or by physical bonding. In chemical bonding, a reaction occurs to make new adhesive molecules. For example, in Super Glue Instant Adhesive, smaller adhesive molecules combine to form longer chains of molecules that react with the surface being bonded. In physical bonding, an adhesive wets two surfaces by forming a thin layer of liquid between two solids.

Since the liquid touches both surfaces everywhere, when it dries, it holds the solids together.

There are several types of physical bonding. With an evaporative adhesive, evaporation leaves behind a dried layer that holds the solids together. For example, white glue found in squeeze bottles is normally made of poly(vinyl acetate), PVA, in water. When this white glue is placed between two porous solids such as wood or paper, the water leaves and the PVA remains to hold the solids together.

With hot adhesives, a hot, melted adhesive wets two surfaces by forming a thin layer of liquid between them. When the liquid cools, it forms a seal that locks the two surfaces together. Your cola-glue when applied hot works in this way—just like a hot glue gun.

Project Ideas and Further Investigations

- With an adult's help, repeat this experiment with different types of regular carbonated soft drinks. Keep track of the heating conditions such as temperature and time. Try to determine how thick to make the hot syrup to make the best glue. How do the glues made from different drinks compare?
- With an adult's help, dissolve 4 tablespoons of sugar in 1/2 cup of water, then repeat the experiment using this sugar and water mixture. Boil until most of the water is gone and then test the glue. Does this sugar and water mixture make glue that is as strong as the cola glue? Can you explain why?

Chapter 4

CHANGES: FREEZING, BOILING, AND MORE

Many different substances can go through physical or chemical changes. For example, when carbon dioxide gas leaves a liquid, it is a physical change because no new substance is formed. In a chemical change, a new substance is created.

Boiling is a type of physical change. While the form of the substance changes, no new substance is made. At a high enough temperature (the boiling point), liquid completely changes to a gas. At a low enough temperature (the freezing point), liquid changes to a solid. Boiling and freezing points can increase when pressure increases. Under normal pressure, pure water boils at 100°C (212°F) and freezes at 0°C (32°F). If the pressure is increased, such as in a pressure cooker, the boiling point increases—the water reaches temperatures higher than 2 100°C (212°F). Adding substances to a liquid can also change the boiling and freezing points of the liquid. In a mixture such as sugar water, for example, the freezing point is lower and the boiling point is higher than for the pure liquid.

In a boiling liquid, bubbles of gas form and escape from the liquid's surface. In a carbonated beverage, bubbles can form at room temperature. Just because there are bubbles in the beverage does not mean the beverage is boiling. Something different causes the bubbles to form in the drink. Under pressure, water molecules surround CO_2 gas. Whenever a bottle or can of carbonated soda is opened, the volume of the dissolved CO_2 increases, and the gas makes bubbles and escapes from the liquid. When a carbonated beverage is bubbling, you know that CO_2 is leaving the liquid.

An example of a chemical change is the formation of rust. Rust is a combination of iron, oxygen, and water. Rust is a different substance than any of the original substances. Acids can react with rust and other metal oxides to cause further chemical changes to occur.

In this chapter, you will use soda pop to explore physical and chemical changes. You will examine how adding sugar to water can affect the freezing point and boiling point, explore how salt can be used to make bubbles of carbon dioxide form, and determine what effect the acid in cola has on metal oxides.

LOWERING FREEZING POINT

In this experiment you will try to determine if cola has a lower freezing point than water. In addition, you will determine how the amount of sugar in cola compares to pure water and to corn syrup and how this affects its freezing point.

Materials

* measuring cup
* 3 clear, disposable plastic cups
* water
* cola
* corn syrup
* freezer
* watch or clock

Pour $1/2$ cup of water into a clear plastic cup. Place $1/2$ cup of cola (not diet) into a second plastic cup. Add $1/2$ cup of corn syrup to a third cup. Place the three cups in a freezer (see Figure 13).

Check the cups each hour for five hours and then check after they have been in the freezer for a total of at least 24 hours. When you check a cup, tilt it to the side and observe if there is liquid, solid, or both present. Corn syrup is a viscous (slow-flowing) liquid, so you may have to wait 10 to 30 seconds to see if it is flowing when you tilt the corn syrup cup. When you check the cups, also touch the top of the water, cola, and syrup to see how each one feels. As soon as you are finished observing each cup, immediately return it to the freezer. In your science notebook, record the total time in the freezer and your observations for each liquid.

The temperature of freezers varies somewhat, but freezers are always set below the freezing point of water. Water freezes at 0°C (32°F). A typical temperature for a freezer is about –7°C (20°F).

At this low temperature, would you expect water to change from a liquid to solid? How long did it take for the water to freeze? Water freezes at the top first, and then the rest of the water freezes into one solid piece.

Did the corn syrup remain a liquid even after 24 hours in the freezer? Corn syrup is thick and viscous because it has many sugar molecules dissolved in water. The sugar molecules cause the water to have a lower freezing point. Molecules added to water make it more difficult for the water molecules to form a solid. If the corn syrup has a freezing point below the temperature of your freezer, then it will remain a liquid.

Figure 13. Place cups with water, cola, and corn syrup in a freezer. Check the cups after 1, 2, 3, 4, 5, and 24 hours to see if the liquids have frozen solid.

Colas are usually sweetened with either fructose sugar molecules made from corn syrup or sucrose sugar molecules. Which would you expect to have a lower freezing point—water or cola? Which took longer to freeze in your experiment—water, cola, or corn syrup? Did the cola freeze? Did the corn syrup freeze? Do you think cola or corn syrup has more sugar molecules?

Project Idea and Further Investigation

Repeat this experiment using cups containing pure water, water with known amounts of sugar, regular soft drinks, and diet soft drinks. Use several different types of soft drinks. Record your observations about how long it takes the liquids to freeze to a solid and how they look. Do the diet drinks behave more like the water or like the sugar-containing soft drinks? Can you explain why?

RAISING BOILING POINT

By doing this experiment you will determine the boiling point of water and cola. The object is to find how the sugar in cola affects the temperature at which water boils. Make a table in your science notebook with columns labeled *Time (minutes)*, *Water Temperature (°F)*, and *Cola Temperature (°F)*.

Have an adult help you with this experiment. Fill an empty 500-mL plastic bottle with water until it is at the same level as the liquid in an unopened 500-mL bottle of cola. You now have equal amounts of water and cola. Pour all the water from the bottle into a metal pan. Clip a candy thermometer on the side of the pan so that the bottom

Materials

* an adult
* empty 500-mL plastic bottle (16- or 20-oz bottles could also be used)
* plastic half-liter bottle of cola (500-mL)
* water
* metal pan—at least 10 cm (4 in) deep
* candy thermometer with clip
* stove
* watch or kitchen timer

of the thermometer is in the water but is not touching the bottom of the pan (see Figure 14). Now place the pan containing the water and thermometer on the stove. Observe the temperature on the thermometer. The candy thermometer will probably be in units Fahrenheit, but if it is Celsius then record the temperatures in °C.

Figure 14. To monitor the temperature of the liquid you are heating, clip a candy thermometer on the side of the pan. The bottom of the thermometer should not touch the pan's bottom.

In the table in your science notebook, record the time as 0 and write the temperature of the water.

Ask an adult to turn the stove unit on a medium-high setting. Start the timer on the watch. Every two minutes record the total time and the temperature of the water. Continue to record the time and temperature for up to 50 minutes or until the water has been boiling for at least 10 minutes. If the water begins to boil too vigorously, **ask the adult** to reduce the stove unit heat setting, but keep the water boiling.

When you are finished collecting your data, ask an adult to turn off the stove. Wait for the water to cool. Remove the candy thermometer and pour out the water. Now repeat this procedure using 500 mL of cola in place of the water. Record the temperatures every two minutes as you did before. After the temperature remains steady for about ten minutes, stop the experiment. If you continue to heat the soda too long, the temperature will begin to rise again. If the temperature continues to rise after you have reached the initial boiling point, then you need to stop the experiment. Excessive heating causes water molecules to leave and the remaining liquid becomes more concentrated.

After you have collected all your data, use graph paper or a computer spreadsheet program to make a plot of temperature versus time (see Figure 15). Ask an adult to help you if you need it.

Did the water temperature rise and then level off? The reading at which the temperature levels off at the top of your graph is called the boiling point. What did you find for the boiling point of water? Water is expected to boil at 100°C (212°F) at sea level. If you are at a higher elevation, the boiling point of the water is lower because there is less air pressure pushing on the surface of the water. Also, since the thermometer you are using may not be exact, you may

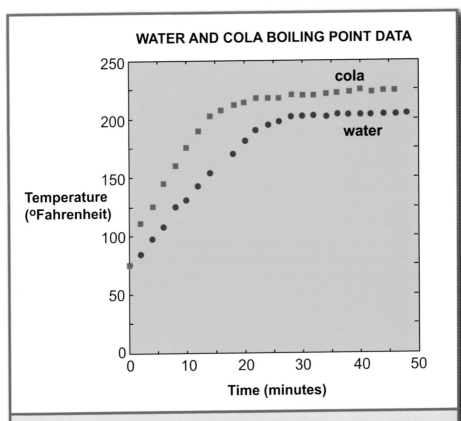

WATER AND COLA BOILING POINT DATA

Temperature (°Fahrenheit)

Time (minutes)

Figure 15. Make a plot of temperature versus time of heating for water and cola. At the boiling point, the temperature stops rising and remains steady.

find a boiling point for water that is a little different than 100°C (212°F).

Did the cola temperature rise and then level off? Did the cola level off at a higher temperature than the water? While the cola boils, the temperature should remain at a fixed value. What was the boiling point of the cola?

When pure water or a sugar water mixture boils, water molecules leave the liquid and go into the gas (vapor) phase. The molecules change from liquid to gas and spread into the room air. The bubbles that are seen in boiling water are small pockets of hot gaseous water molecules rising to the surface of the liquid.

Because cola is sweetened with either fructose or sucrose sugar molecules made from corn syrup or sucrose sugar molecules, it has a higher boiling point than pure water. A sugar and water mixture is expected to boil above 100°C (212°F) at sea level. The more sugar in the mixture, the higher the temperature required to boil the mixture.

Project Ideas and Further Investigations

Have an adult help you with any further experiments requiring the use of the stove.

- Repeat this experiment using diet cola. Since diet cola does not contain sugar, do you expect its boiling point to be closer to that of water or of regular cola? What do you observe?
- Repeat this experiment with various soft drinks. Make a table that compares the boiling point to the amount of sugar listed on the product labels. Does more sugar cause a higher boiling point in all drinks?

CREATING BUBBLES WITH SALT

In this experiment you will find out if salt and other solids can be used to test for dissolved carbon dioxide.

Materials

* unopened bottle of cola
* bowl
* clock or timer
* salt shaker

Open a bottle of cola and gently pour it into a bowl until it is about an inch deep. Wait about 30 seconds until any foam has cleared from the top of the liquid. Sprinkle salt from a salt shaker on top of the liquid in the bowl. What happens? Do you hear fizzing and see bubbles forming?

Wait about 30 seconds more and then sprinkle salt on the cola again. Repeat this activity as many times as you choose. Are bubbles formed every time? How many times can you sprinkle salt and see a cloud of bubbles form?

Carbonated drinks have carbon dioxide gas dissolved in the liquid. This carbon dioxide will slowly come out of the soda pop if the soda is left open to the air. You can test any carbonated soda to see if it still has dissolved gas in it or if it has lost its dissolved carbon dioxide and gone flat. Sprinkle salt in a small sample of the soda you wish to test and observe if any bubbles form.

When pure water or a sugar water mixture boils, water molecules leave the liquid and go into the gas phase. The molecules change from liquid molecules to become gas molecules that spread into the room air. The bubbles that are seen in boiling water are small pockets of hot gaseous water molecules rising to the surface of the liquid. Hot liquids including water can boil up suddenly if small amounts of solid particles are added. **DO NOT SPRINKLE SALT OR SOLID PARTICLES ON A HOT LIQUID.**

In this experiment, the small particles of salt provide surfaces where gas can collect and larger bubbles can form. This process of providing sites for other gases or molecules to collect is called nucleation. Carbon dioxide molecules gather on the surface of the salt and form larger bubbles of gas that rise to the top of the liquid.

Nucleation is sometimes used to try to make it rain in a process called cloud seeding. There are several different methods of seeding clouds. In one method, a plane is used to drop small particles of silver iodide into a cloud where the temperature is below 0°C (32°F). The cold water vapor in the cloud will form ice crystals on the solid particles, and the ice crystals fall to the earth. On the way to the ground, the ice crystals melt and become rain. Cloud seeding does not always work, and some states prohibit it because of fears it may disrupt natural patterns of rainfall.

Project Ideas and Further Investigation

- Repeat the activity above while adding the same amounts of different types of solids such as salt, sugar, baking soda, sand, and pepper. Try different clear carbonated drinks. Make a chart of your results trying different solids and different drinks. Which drinks give the most fizz? Which solids cause the most bubbles to be released?
- Allow different sodas to remain open to the air and test them for fizz several times each day for four days. Make a chart of your results and compare how long it takes for different sodas to lose all their fizz.

Experiment 4.4

REMOVING RUST AND DISSOLVING METAL OXIDES

When a penny is new, it has a shiny copper surface. Pennies minted since 1983 are made of zinc and covered with a thin layer of copper. Over time the penny's copper surface changes to a dull brown. This change in color is due to a layer of copper oxide that forms on the surface. Oxygen from the air combines with copper to make the brown copper oxide. In this experiment, you will find out if you can use cola that contains phosphoric acid in a chemical reaction to remove the copper oxide layer.

Materials

* 3 older brown pennies
* bowl
* cola that contains phosphoric acid
* new shiny penny
* paper towel

Place two older brown pennies—head side up—in a bowl. Cover the pennies with cola about 2.5 cm (1 in) deep. After about 30 minutes turn the pennies over to place them tail side up in the bowl. After about 30 minutes remove the pennies and pour out the cola from the bowl. Be sure to thoroughly clean the bowl at the end of your experiment. Observe the pennies and compare them to the third old brown penny that was not cleaned. Wipe the pennies with a paper towel to dry them. Do the old, cleaned pennies look more like the remaining old one or a new shiny penny?

The cola contains phosphoric acid (H_3PO_4). When copper oxide (CuO) is placed in an acid, copper ions (Cu_2^+) are released and water (H_2O) molecules are formed. ($H_3PO_4 + CuO \rightarrow Cu_2^+ + H_2O$)

The copper oxide layer on an old penny dissolves in acid. As the copper oxide layer is removed, it reveals a clean copper surface underneath.

Project Ideas and Further Investigations

- Repeat this activity using as many different soft drinks as you can find. Some soft drinks contain phosphoric acid, while other drinks contain citric acid. Some drinks contain both phosphoric and citric acids. Is there any difference in cleaning ability between citric acid and phosphoric acid? Is there any difference between diet and regular drinks in cleaning pennies? Try to rate different sodas by their cleaning ability and compare these results to the contents of the drinks.

- Rust is a combination of iron atoms, oxygen atoms, and water molecules. Test and compare different sodas in their ability to remove rust. Find rusted iron or steel objects such as old nails. Or you can make rusted objects by leaving wet iron nails exposed to the air for several days. Place these rusted objects in jars and cover with different sodas. Leave for an hour, then remove the objects and dry with a paper towel. Was the rust removed? Try to rate different sodas in their cleaning ability and compare these results to the contents of the drinks.

Chapter 5

HOLD THAT DRINK: METAL, GLASS, AND PLASTIC

The first containers used for carbonated soft drinks were glass bottles. Many different methods were used to seal these glass bottles until William Painter invented the crown cap in 1892. The crown cap is a metal cap pinched on the top of a glass bottle. It has been used ever since to seal glass bottles containing carbonated beverages. Over the years, carbonated drinks have been sold in glass bottles, metal cans, and plastic bottles. This chapter explores some of the properties of these different types of containers.

Today in the United States, most soft drinks are sold in either plastic bottles or aluminum cans. Metal cans came into widespread use in the 1960s. The modern aluminum drink can is much more than just aluminum. It includes paint on the outside, a plastic liner on the inside, and a lid made of aluminum and magnesium for extra strength. In 1978 Coke was the first drink sold in polyethylene terephthalate (PET, or PETE) plastic bottles.

Soda-lime glass is made by heating together a mixture of silica (SiO_2), soda ash (Na_2CO_3, sodium carbonate), and calcium carbonate ($CaCO_3$). Soda-lime glass becomes soft at about 700°C (1300°F), and the softened glass can be molded into shapes, such as a bottle.

Soda-lime glass can be clear and colorless. However, impurities in the glass can add color. For example, if there is iron oxide present, it can make the glass green.

Aluminum is lightweight and strong and is the most abundant metal in the earth's crust. The process used to make aluminum from bauxite ore was developed in 1886 by a young college student named Charles Hall and is called the Hall process. Prior to the development of the Hall process, aluminum was a very expensive metal—more valuable than gold.

In this chapter you will explore the design of plastic bottles that must be able to hold the pressure of trapped carbon dioxide gas. You will build your own balance and use it to compare the mass of metal cans, plastic bottles, and glass bottles. Finally, you will compare how fast heat can pass through aluminum, glass, and plastic.

Experiment 5.1
POP A TOP—
HOLDING PRESSURE

Aluminum cans, glass bottles, and plastic bottles are all designed to hold carbonated beverages under pressure until the drink is served. Sealed aluminum cans, glass bottles with metal caps, and plastic bottles with screw-on caps all have to contain the pressure of gas inside the bottle. The pressure inside the bottle may be several times greater than the normal, outside atmospheric pressure.

Materials

* small bowl
* sink with hot water
* unopened bottle of cola
* empty plastic 35mm film canister with pop-on top
* watch or timer
* milk carton with screw-on lid

In this experiment, you will examine what happens when you use a container that is not designed to hold the pressure of a gas. The object of this experiment is to determine how long a film canister with a pop–on top can hold the pressure of gas from a carbonated soda.

Note: The plastic top of a 35mm film canister can safely pop off. Do not use any other type of container for this experiment.

Set a small bowl in a sink and fill it with warm water. Open a bottle of cola and gently pour the cola into an empty plastic film canister. Fill the canister about two-thirds full. Quickly snap the top on the plastic holder. Start a timer or look at the time on a watch. Shake the canister back and forth about five times and then place

Pressure increases.
Lid pops and gas escapes.

Figure 16. If enough carbon dioxide gas bubbles out of the liquid, the pressure increases enough to push the lid off the film canister.

it in the bowl of warm water. Observe the film canister. Did the top pop off? How long did it take?

Repeat this activity six more times. Average the times required for the top to pop off. The cap may not pop off every time, either because gas leaks out or because the pressure does not rise high enough.

Carbon dioxide gas from a carbonated soda will escape into the surrounding air unless held inside a sealed container. When the cap is placed on the film holder and shaken and warmed, it causes more gas to bubble out of the cola. If the pressure of this gas increases enough, it forces the top off the film canister (see Figure 16).

Repeat the experiment using cold water in the bowl and compare the results. Repeat the experiment in warm and cold water with no shaking of the sealed canister. Compare how long it takes for the top to pop off under these four conditions: warm and shaken, cold and shaken, warm and not shaken, and cold and not shaken. Under what conditions is the top most likely to stay on the canister?

Unscrew a milk carton top. Unscrew a soda bottle top. How much did you have to turn each cap before it came off? Look closely at the necks of the bottles where the tops are screwed down. Do you see one ridge on the neck of the milk bottle? Do you see three ridges on the neck of the soda bottle? What do these ridges have to do with how many turns were required to remove each bottle top? Next compare each of the tops. Is the milk top flat and wide? Is the soda top tall and narrow? Why would a milk bottle not be a good design for holding a carbonated beverage and its carbon dioxide gas pressure?

Project Idea and Further Investigation

Repeat the experiment for as many different carbonated drinks as possible. Compare the times required to pop the top for these different drinks. Keep the caps on the soda bottles when you are not pouring out any liquid.

WATCHING WEIGHT— A COMPARISON OF SOLIDS

Aluminum cans, glass bottles, and plastic bottles are used to deliver carbonated beverages to people around the world. Whether aluminum, glass, or plastic, the container must be strong enough to hold the pressure of the carbon dioxide gas sealed inside. Can you think of some advantages to each of these materials? In this experiment, you will make a balance. You will use it to compare the weight of glass, plastic, and aluminum required to hold the same amount of a carbonated beverage. The object of this experiment is to determine which material—aluminum, glass, or plastic—requires the least weight to hold the same amount of a carbonated drink.

Assemble your balance as shown in Figure 17. Tie identical 51-cm-(20-in-) long strings at the 12-, 18- and 24-in marks on the yardstick. Tape each string to the yardstick so that the strings will not slide out of position. Tie plastic bags to

Materials

* 3 pieces of string, each 51 cm (20 in) long
* yardstick
* tape
* 2 light plastic bags (such as type used to bag groceries)
* 2×2-inch board, 4 feet (1.2 m) long
* 2 kitchen chairs
* nickel, or modeling clay
* empty glass soda bottle (8-oz size)
* 20 empty aluminum soda cans (12-oz size)
* empty plastic soda bottle (16.9-oz, 0.5-liter size)

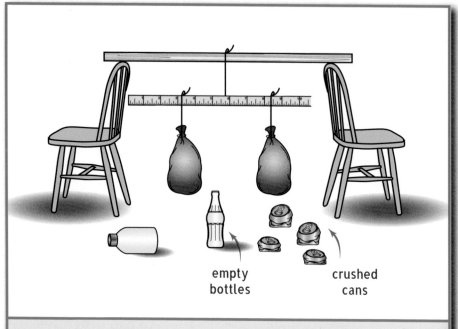

empty
bottles

crushed
cans

Figure 17. Two plastic bags tied with string to a yardstick that is held by another string make a useful balance. You can use your balance to compare the masses of the object or objects in the two bags.

the strings at the 12-in and 24-in positions. Then tie the string at the 18-in mark to a board suspended between two chairs.

Look at the balance you have made. If the yardstick is not level, tape a nickel at a spot somewhere along the stick to balance the two sides (or you can add a piece of modeling clay to level the stick). Make sure the yardstick is level, not tilted to one side or the other, before continuing.

Place one empty 8-oz glass bottle in the bag on the left of your balance. The yardstick will now be tilted steeply to the left. Next add empty 12-oz aluminum cans, one at a time, to the bag on the right side of your balance. You may need to crush or flatten the cans so that they take up less room in the bag. Continue adding cans until the right side weighs as much as the left side (the yardstick is level) or weighs just slightly more (the yardstick is tilted to the right). Record the number of cans used.

Remove the bottle and all the cans from the bags. As you did before, make sure the balance with empty bags is level. If not balanced, move the nickel or modeling clay to balance the two sides.

Place one empty 16.9-oz (0.5-liter) plastic bottle in the left bag. Next add empty 12-oz aluminum cans, one at a time, to the bag on the right side of your balance. Continue adding cans until the right side weighs just as much as the left side (the yardstick is level) or weighs just slightly more (the yardstick is tilted to the right). Record the number of cans required to balance the plastic bottle. Estimate a fraction if it is more than one number but less than the next.

An empty aluminum drink can has a mass of about 14 g. Multiply this mass by the number of aluminum cans required to balance the glass bottle and the number of cans to balance the plastic bottle. How do the weights (or masses) of these three containers compare? How much mass of aluminum, plastic, or glass would you need to hold 16 oz (473 mL) of soda drink?

If you have access to a quantitative balance in a school laboratory, you can weigh the three containers and compare the readings to the results you found.

Project Ideas and Further Investigations

- Repeat this experiment but use nickels to balance the weight of an empty aluminum can. Then use nickels to balance an empty plastic bottle and finally to balance an empty glass bottle. Multiply the number of nickels used for each container times 5 g to determine the actual weight of an aluminum can, plastic bottle, and glass bottle.

- Place a regular unopened cola can in the left bag of your balance and an unopened diet cola can in the right bag. Which is heavier? Add pennies to the bag with the diet cola can until the two sides are balanced. Pennies made since 1983 weigh 2.5 g. Assuming everything else about the two cans is the same, this mass gives a rough estimate of the amount of sugar in the regular cola. Your result may tend to underestimate the amount of sugar. Compare your result to the grams of sugar listed on the cola can label. For another way to determine sugar contents, see Experiment 1.1.

SPEED OF HEAT FLOW

Does heat flow faster through a plastic bottle, glass bottle, or aluminum can? The object of this experiment is to measure and compare the speed of heat flow through three different solids and through different amounts of material.

Set an empty aluminum can, plastic bottle, and glass bottle on the counter next to a sink. Turn the sink faucet to hot and let the water run for several minutes until it is as hot as it will get. Place a large bowl in the sink, and fill it with hot water.

Use a butter knife to cut off a piece of cold butter about the size of a penny and about 0.5 cm (1/4 in) thick. Use the knife to stick this piece of butter onto the outside of the can, about 2.5 cm (1 in) from the bottom. Put a funnel in the can, and quickly pour exactly one cup of hot water into the can. As soon as the water is in the can, have your partner start a watch or timer. When the butter slides to the bottom of the can, stop the timer and record the time.

Materials

* empty cola can
* empty plastic cola bottle
* empty glass cola bottle
* sink with hot water
* large bowl
* butter knife
* stick of butter
* funnel
* liquid measuring cup
* partner
* watch or timer
* paper towel
* refrigerator

Repeat this procedure using the same amount of butter on the plastic bottle. Record the time the butter remains before it slips off. Repeat the procedure on the glass bottle. Record the observed time.

Pour the water out of the can, plastic bottle, and glass bottle. Wipe the butter off the outside of the containers. Put the rest of the butter back into the refrigerator. Wait about 15 minutes for the containers to cool to room temperature. Repeat the experiment for the can, plastic bottle, and glass bottle and record the observed times.

Once again pour out the water, wipe off the outsides, wait 15 minutes, and repeat the experiment. Record all the times.

Find the average time for each different type of solid. What was the average time for the butter to slide off the aluminum, the glass, and the plastic?

Scientists have found that heat always flows from the hotter side to the colder side of an object. Atoms in a solid are never perfectly still. As they vibrate back and forth, they can pass on their motion or heat energy to nearby atoms. The hot water poured inside each container causes the inside to be warmer than the outside. Heat flows from the hotter inside to the colder outside (see Figure 18).

When the heat reaches the butter, the part of solid butter touching the surface melts, and the butter slides off. The sliding butter provides a way to measure how quickly the outside of the container becomes warm.

The rate of heat conduction (heat passing through a solid) depends on both the substance and its thickness. For the same thickness we expect heat conduction to be fastest in metal and slowest in plastic. However, heat can move more quickly through a thin solid than a thick one. Can you use these facts to explain your observations?

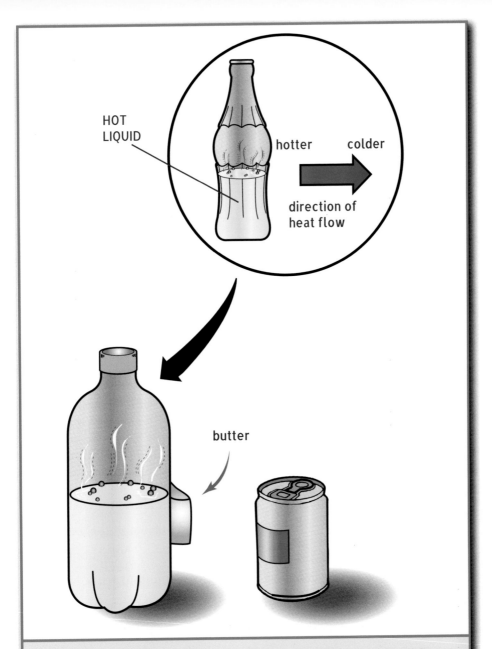

HOT LIQUID

hotter   colder

direction of heat flow

butter

Figure 18. Heat always flows from the hotter side to the colder side of an object. As atoms in a solid vibrate, they pass on energy of motion (heat) to nearby atoms that have less energy. In this way heat energy spreads throughout a solid.

To understand the transfer of heat in three different materials, you need to know something about the structures of the materials. Metal atoms can vibrate and jostle nearby atoms. Metals also contain some free electrons that can move and help conduct heat and electricity. In a plastic, the atoms are locked in place as part of large molecules called polymers, and they are not able to effectively transfer heat. Glass is made of different types of solids melted together. Glass does not conduct heat nearly as fast as a metal.

Project Ideas and Further Investigations

- To explore how the thickness of a solid affects heat flow, use four empty aluminum cans and a roll of 30-cm- (12-in-) wide aluminum foil. From the roll of aluminum foil, cut a piece that is 229 cm (90 in) long. Fold this piece in thirds lengthwise so that you have a triple-thickness piece that is still 90 in long but now just 10 cm (4 in) wide. Now cut this long piece into four smaller pieces that are 23, 46, 69, and 92 cm (9, 18, 27, and 36 in) long.

  Wrap each piece of foil around an empty aluminum can. Place a rubber band around the top and bottom of the foil on each can to tightly hold the aluminum in place. You should now have cans that have one, two, three, and four triple layers of aluminum around them. In other words, the cans have 3, 6, 9, and 12 layers of aluminum around them. Repeat the original experiment with butter and hot water for each can. Time how long the butter will stick on each can. How does the thickness of the aluminum foil affect the speed of heat conduction from the hot water out to the butter? Prepare a chart of your results.

- Repeat the original experiment using drinking glasses or other containers of as close to the same thickness as you can find. Use containers made of metal, glass, and plastic. How long does it take for the butter to slide off each type of solid? How does the speed of heat conduction compare to your original experiment? Does the plastic or glass take longer to conduct heat?

Chapter 6

SODA SENSATIONS: Smell and Taste

There are five human senses: smell, taste, touch, hearing, and sight. Of these five senses, smell and taste are the most closely related. Most of how something tastes is really due to the way it smells. In this chapter you will explore how taste and smell work together when you drink carbonated beverages.

The tongue is covered with tiny taste buds. Nerve fibers carry signals from the taste buds to the brain. Different sections of the tongue transmit different types of taste. There are four well-known tastes—sweet, sour, salty, and bitter—but scientists have discovered other tastes such as metallic, chalky, and umami (a meaty taste). Root beer and grape soda are both sweet to the tongue, but their unique tastes are due to odor molecules they contain. The sense of smell gives each food its true distinct flavor.

Between your eyes, behind the bridge of your nose, and inside each of your two nasal passages is a dime-sized spot called the olfactory epithelium (see Figure 19a). The olfactory epithelium contains about 20 million olfactory neurons (nerve cells). Olfactory nerves go through the bones of the skull to connect with a part of the brain called the olfactory bulb (see Figure 19b).

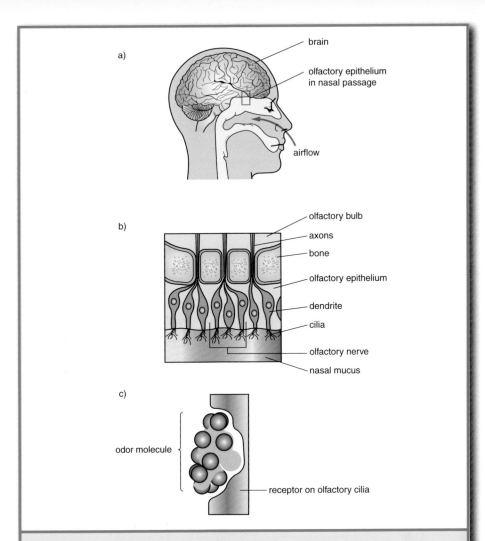

a) brain

olfactory epithelium
in nasal passage

airflow

b) olfactory bulb

axons

bone

olfactory epithelium

dendrite

cilia

olfactory nerve

nasal mucus

c)

odor molecule

receptor on olfactory cilia

Figure 19. a) The olfactory epithelium is at the top of each nasal passage. b) The olfactory epithelium is lined with special nerve cells whose branched dendrite ends are covered with cilia and bathed with mucus. The long axons of the olfactory receptor nerve cells extend through the skull into the olfactory bulb. c) The tiny cilia contain olfactory protein receptor sites into which selected odor molecules can fit and trigger electric impulses. The olfactory bulb receives these nerve impulses, organizes them, and allows the brain to interpret specific molecules as having unique odors.

Odor molecules from the air dissolve in the slimy mucus that covers the olfactory receptor neurons. Odor molecules bind along the cilia at the ends of olfactory nerve cells (see Figure 19c).

Among the 20 million different olfactory neurons, there are about 1,000 different types. Each neuron has one type of receptor on it. A collection of specific odor molecules will fit into only some of these 1,000 different types of olfactory receptors. If odor molecules fit into the receptors on a neuron, a signal is sent to the olfactory bulb. The brain then interprets each unique signal pattern as a smell. Root beer and grape soda smell different to you because they each have a different collection of molecules that go into your nose. Odor molecules get into the air, enter the olfactory epithelium, bind at specific sites on neurons, and cause signals to be generated that the brain recognizes as a specific odor. You sniff and your brain thinks either "grape soda" or "root beer."

In this chapter there are experiments that explore the effect of time on the taste of a carbonated soda, using smell to identify drinks, influencing taste with odors, and measuring the threshold of taste.

Experiment 6.1
TASTING TIME

Have you ever tasted a carbonated drink that had gone flat—lost all its dissolved carbon dioxide gas? How did it taste? In this experiment, you will explore if people can use their ability to detect carbonation to determine how long a drink has been opened. You will do this experiment over three days, and you should do your work at about the same time each day. The object of this experiment is to determine if you can identify how long a drink has been opened by the amount of carbonation remaining.

Materials

* 3 cans of cola
* 3 glasses
* marker
* masking tape
* refrigerator
* 6 small disposable paper cups
* partner

On the first day, open a can of cola and pour it into a clean glass. Write *2 Days Old* on a piece of masking tape, and stick this tape on the glass. Set this glass where it will not be disturbed in the refrigerator.

On the second day, open a can of cola and pour it into another clean glass. Write *1 Day Old* on a piece of masking tape, and stick this tape on the glass. Set this glass with the first one. Place a third can of cola, unopened, in the refrigerator.

On the third day, open the can of cola that has been in the refrigerator overnight and pour it into a clean glass. Write *Fresh* on a piece of tape and stick this tape on the glass. Pour some of each drink into one of three small paper cups. Label the cups *2 Days, 1 Day*, and *Fresh* (see Figure 20).

Close your eyes and have a partner hand you the cups one at a time in no special order. Sip a small amount of the cola in each cup. As you taste each of the cups of cola, identify the ones that have the most to the least fizz. Record how well your sense of taste was able to place the drinks in order from oldest to freshest cola.

Switch places with your partner, get three unused paper cups for the drinks, and allow your partner to try each drink with his or her eyes closed. If possible, have other volunteers taste the drinks and place them in order. You can change the conditions of this experiment by starting a new glass every 12 hours instead of every 24.

Figure 20. If left opened, the taste of soda drinks changes with time because carbonation is lost. Can you tell which cola has been opened the longest?

Carbonated water has a much different taste than pure water. The taste of carbonation changes with the amount of carbon dioxide dissolved in the water. Could you and others tell which drink had lost the most carbonation and was the oldest? Were you able to use taste to tell how much time had passed?

Project Idea and Further Investigation

Open two small (such as 500-mL size) plastic bottles of cola. Pour half the cola from the first bottle into a drinking glass. Pour half the cola from the second bottle into a drinking glass. Screw the caps on each bottle. Use masking tape and a marker to label one bottle and glass *Cold*. Place this closed bottle and open glass in a refrigerator. Use masking tape and a marker to label the other bottle and glass *Warm*. Place this closed bottle and open glass out in the room.

After 12 hours, pour samples into four paper cups. Label the four cups *Cold—Closed, Cold—Opened, Warm—Closed*, and *Warm—Opened*. Wait about 15 minutes for the cold liquid to come to room temperature. As in the original experiment, taste the four colas with your eyes closed and with the help of a partner. Record your results. Place the samples in order from most to least carbonation. Repeat the testing after 24 hours. What is the best way to have the cola retain its carbonation and not go flat?

IDENTIFYING DRINKS BY ODOR

Humans and animals have the ability to identify many foods by smell. This ability is important to the survival of many animals. In this activity, you will explore how well people can identify some common soft drinks by smell alone.

Materials

* drinks in plastic bottles including Coke, Pepsi, Sprite, root beer, grape soda, Mello Yello, and ginger ale.
* 6 volunteers

Set up a page in your science notebook that lists the seven different drinks, and a column for the drink identification given by each of the six volunteers (see Figure 21). Have the first volunteer sit in a room and show her the seven bottles that will be used. Ask her to close her eyes and keep them closed. Open the first bottle and hold it just beneath your volunteer's nose. Ask her to identify what she smells, and then close that bottle. Record her choice beside the correct drink name in your science notebook. Continue until all seven drinks have been tested. Do not present the drinks in any special order.

Repeat this experiment with additional volunteers. In your science notebook, record the answers from each volunteer. Make a new column of results for each volunteer.

When you have completed testing all the volunteers, compare their answers. How many items did each volunteer correctly identify? Were some of the drink odors more difficult to identify? What drinks were easier to identify?

When an odor signal reaches the brain, if it is a unique odor with a distinct smell, the brain will have an easier time distinguishing it. If the odor is one that the person commonly smells, the person will have a strong memory of that smell and it will be easier for the person to remember.

Humans may be able to distinguish (tell apart) up to 10,000 different odors. However, identifying a unique odor is more difficult than distinguishing between two odors. To identify a smell, you must know a name that goes with it and not just that it is different from another odor. Although people can distinguish between thousands of different smells, the average person can probably name and identify only a few hundred specific odors. However, some people, such as those who work preparing new perfume mixtures, have been trained to recognize thousands of different odors.

Drink Identification by Smell			
Drink	Volunteer 1 identifies	Volunteer 2 identifies	Volunteer 3 identifies
Coke			
Pepsi			
Sprite			
Root Beer			
Grape Soda			
Mello Yello			
Ginger Ale			

Figure 21. Make a chart with a list of all the drinks and record each drink your volunteers report that they smell

Project Idea and Further Investigation

Try increasing the number of different drinks to smell. Add other non-carbonated drinks such as milk, orange juice, and different flavored sports drinks. Continue to try to find which drinks are easiest to identify by smell and which ones are most difficult. Is it possible for your volunteers to distinguish different types of the same category drink—such as different brands of root beer or different brands of cola?

Experiment 6.3
A Tasty Smell

Is the flavor of a food or drink due to smell or taste or both? In this experiment you will try to sort out the contribution from each of these senses. The object is to determine if the smell of one soda can cause a person to "taste" that soda while drinking a different one.

Materials

* several volunteers
* drinks in plastic bottles, including lemon-lime soda, root beer, grape soda, and cola
* straws
* cups

Have a partner sit with his eyes closed. Hold a freshly opened bottle of root beer just below his nose. Then hand your partner a straw that is placed in a bottle of lemon-lime soda farther from his nose (see Figure 22). Have him take one sip of lemon-lime soda. Ask him what type of soda he drank.

Wait a minute and repeat this activity with the next drink. Allow him to smell grape soda while taking one sip of lemon-lime soda. Wait a minute and then have him smell cola while taking a sip of lemon-lime soda. After each taste test, record what your volunteer smelled, what he actually drank, and what he reported that he drank.

Lemon-lime soda has a sweet taste, but the aroma of the other drinks may dominate and make him think that what he smelled was actually in his mouth. What a person "tastes" is mostly due to what he or she smells. Did your partner report that he was drinking lemon-lime soda or that he was drinking what he smelled? Repeat with additional volunteers (and fresh straws and sodas).

Molecules can reach the olfactory epithelium through the nose (orthonasal passageway) or from the mouth through the back of the throat (retronasal passageway; see Figure 23). When eating or drinking, odors traveling through the retronasal passageway usually dominate over odors traveling directly through the nose. However, in this experiment, if enough odor molecules go through the nose, then that scent may overwhelm the odor of what is in the mouth. In this case what you smell may also be what you "taste."

Figure 22. What do you taste if you sip one drink while smelling another drink?

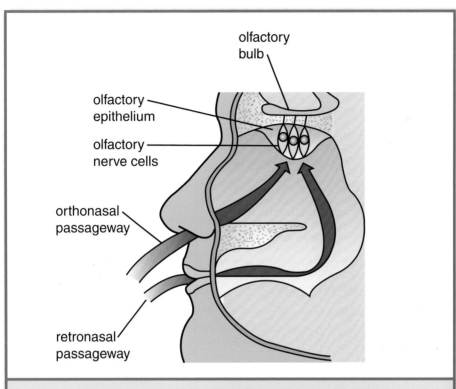

olfactory bulb

olfactory epithelium

olfactory nerve cells

orthonasal passageway

retronasal passageway

Figure 23. The olfactory epithelium is the spot where odor molecules are detected. Odor molecules can reach the olfactory epithelium through the nose (orthonasal passageway) or from the mouth through the back of the throat (retronasal passageway).

Project Idea and Further Investigation

Prepare five mixtures of cups of lemon-lime soda and grape soda in the following amounts: 1 and 0, 3/4 and 1/4, 1/2 and 1/2, 1/4 and 3/4, and 0 and 1. Ask volunteers to identify each drink. Do not tell your volunteers what has been mixed together. Which drinks do they identify as lemon-lime soda and which as grape soda? Are they able to tell it is a mixture? Does the odor of one drink dominate the odor of the other?

TASTE THRESHOLD

A taste threshold is the minimum amount needed to detect the presence of something. When you taste a cola drink, you are detecting a complicated mixture of tastes and odors. The object of this experiment is to find the taste threshold for cola dissolved in water.

Materials

* 7 drinking glasses
* cola
* water
* 7 spoons
* liquid measuring cup
* 4 volunteers
* 56 small disposable paper cups

Add $1/2$ cup of cola and $1/2$ cup of water to a glass and stir. This glass is a $1/2$ dilution of the original cola. Pour $1/2$ cup of the cola from the first glass and $1/2$ cup of water into a second glass and stir. Use a new spoon for each glass. Pour $1/2$ cup of the cola from the second glass and $1/2$ cup of water into a third glass and stir. Pour $1/2$ cup of the cola from the third glass and $1/2$ cup of water into a fourth glass and stir. Pour $1/2$ cup of the cola from the fourth glass and $1/2$ cup of water into a fifth glass and stir. Pour $1/2$ cup of the cola from the fifth glass and $1/2$ cup of water into a sixth glass and stir. Finally, pour $1/2$ cup of cola from the sixth glass and $1/2$ cup of water into a seventh glass and stir.

You should have $1/2$ cup of diluted cola in glasses one through six and one cup in glass seven. The cola color should get lighter as you go from the first to seventh glass. From first through seventh, the glasses contain the following dilutions of the original cola: $1/2$, $1/4$, $1/8$, $1/16$, $1/32$, $1/64$, and $1/128$.

In your science notebook, set up a chart to record your observations (see Figure 24). Pour a small amount of cola from each glass into seven paper cups. Have a volunteer taste the cola in each cup starting with the seventh and going to the first. After she sips the drink in each cup, ask her what she tastes. Repeat this process with other volunteers. Later, have the same volunteers do this activity in order from the first to the seventh cup. Record all the results in your chart.

What was the least amount of cola your volunteers could taste? Did different people have different taste thresholds? Did it make a difference if the cola dilutions were presented from strongest to

Results of Taste Threshold Detection

Glass	Cola Dilution	Volunteer 1 Tasted	Volunteer 2 Tasted	Volunteer 3 Tasted	Volunteer 4 Tasted
1	$1/2$	cola	cola	cola	cola
2	$1/4$	cola	cola	cola	cola
3	$1/8$	cola	cola	cola	cola
4	$1/16$	cola	cola	cola	water
5	$1/32$	water	water	water	water
6	$1/64$	water	water	water	water
7	$1/128$	water	water	water	water

Figure 24. In your science notebook, draw a chart like this one to compare taste thresholds of diluted cola for different volunteers.

weakest or from weakest to strongest? Could you see color from the cola when it could not be tasted?

Project Ideas and Further Investigations

- Add five teaspoons of sugar to exactly one cup of water. Stir until all the sugar is dissolved. This sugar solution has about the same sugar concentration as a typical cola drink. Use this sugar solution in place of the starting cola drink and do the same seven dilutions. Repeat the original experiment using this sugar water. How do the results compare to the original cola taste test?

- Get a bottle of plain (no flavor) seltzer water. Seltzer water, also called carbonated water, is water that has had carbon dioxide gas dissolved in it under pressure. Carbonated water tastes different than regular water due to the dissolved carbon dioxide. Use seltzer water in place of the cola drink and do the same seven dilutions. Repeat the original experiment using these dilutions. How do the results compare to the original cola taste test?

FURTHER READING

Churchill, E. Richard, Louis V. Loeschnig, and Muriel Mandell. *365 Simple Science Experiments With Everyday Materials.* New York: Black Dog & Leventhal Publishers, 2013.

Dutton, Judy. *Science Fair Season: Twelve Kids, a Robot Named Scorch, and What It Takes to Win.* New York: Hyperion Books, 2011.

Editors of TIME for Kids Magazine. *TIME For Kids Big Book of Science Experiments: A Step-by-Step Guide.* New York: TIME for Kids, 2011.

Henneberg, Susan. *Creating Science Fair Projects With Cool New Digital Tools.* New York: Rosen Publishing, 2014.

Margles, Samantha. *Mythbusters Science Fair Book.* New York: Scholastic, 2011.

VanCleave, Janice. *Step-by-Step Science Experiments in Chemistry.* New York: Rosen Publishing, 2013.

Wheeler-Toppen Jodi. *Science Experiments That Fizz and Bubble: Fun Projects for Curious Kids.* Mankato, Minn.: Capstone Press, 2011.

WEB SITES

chem4kids.com

Chemistry for Kids has basic chemistry help and information.

ipl.org/div/projectguide

The IPL's Science Fair Project Resource Guide will help guide you through your science fair project.

leffingwell.com/olfaction.htm

Learn more about the sense of smell.

sciencebuddies.org/science-fair-projects/project_guide_index. shtml

Let Science Buddies give you extra ideas and tips for your science fair project.

INDEX